...he four
...3in machine
...s and six-
...nder cannon
...nted in
...ose of
a Mosquito
Mk.XVIII
'Tsetse'.
BAE Systems
Heritage

Royal Navy
Mosquito FB.Vis
parked at RNAS
Ford, West
Sussex, during
1946. The unit's
FB.VIs were
soon replaced
by TR.33s.
Key Collection

FOREWORD

I f one aircraft epitomises the sheer daring of RAF aircrews during World War Two, it's the de Havilland Mosquito. It was a mount that performed many roles – bomber, night-fighter, fighter-bomber – and undoubtedly it remains legendary due to the audacious ultra-low-level raids performed against targets such as Amiens prison in France, and seemingly almost skimming the waves during Coastal Command attacks on Axis shipping… often running the gauntlet of enemy flak.

Let's not forget the stellar reconnaissance work also conducted by Mosquitos throughout the war, but rubber-stamping its versatility and longevity, the 'Mossie' continued to provide sterling service after the conflict, at home and abroad. It would need to be a capable aircraft to eventually replace the Mosquito, and that transpired as the superb English Electric Canberra, which also excelled in many roles and duly became a 'jet Mosquito'.

This seventh volume of Combat Machines is a fitting and timely vehicle to describe the de Havilland Mosquito, what with Airfix's all-new 1/72 B.XVI kit now being available. But besides this, modellers have many other products for replicating the 'Mossie' in different scales, and these too are explored here besides chapters on the real machine. I'm sure you'll agree that accomplished aviation historians Tony Buttler and Malcolm V Lowe have provided a superb study of the Mosquito across the variants, encompassing its fascinating and ground-breaking design, operations and achievements.

As with all volumes in the Combat Machines series, we aim to provide high-quality reference for aviation enthusiasts and modellers alike, and I hope we've achieved that for you once more.

Chris Clifford
Series Editor

A 4,000lb
'Cookie'
blockbuster
bomb is rolled
on its trolley
underneath a
Mosquito to be
loaded for the
next sortie.
Key Collection

Acknowledgements: Tony Buttler wishes to thank Ian Thirsk and Graham Pitchfork for their help with research and imagery.
Authors: Tony Buttler AMRAeS, Malcolm V Lowe
Series Editor: Chris Clifford
Senior Editor – Bookazines and Specials: Roger Mortimer
roger.mortimer@keypublishing.com

Colour profiles: Andy Hay – Flying Art
Walk Around photos: Jamie Ewan
Designer: Tom Bagley
Head of Publishing: Finbar O'Reilly
Chief Publishing officer: Jonathan Jackson
Head of Production: Janet Watkins
Head of Design: Steve Donovan
Publisher: Mark Elliott
Group CEO: Adrian Cox

Key Publishing Ltd: PO Box 100, Stamford, Lincolnshire, PE9 1XQ, United Kingdom.
Distributed by: Seymour Distribution Ltd, 2 Poultry Avenue, London, EC1A 9PP.
Tel: 020 7429 4000.
Printed by: Precision Colour Print, Telford.
Printed in England
ISBN: 9781-913295-509

CATCH ME IF YOU CAN!....

A lovely air-to-air view of the photo-recce Mosquito prototype W4051. Key Collection

A famous photo showing the first Mosquito prototype, carrying the official military serial W4050, taking off from Hatfield for a test flight on January 10, 1941. BAE Systems Heritage

In World War Two, the great majority of Britain's military aircraft were built in metal but there was one notable exception…the de Havilland (DH) Mosquito. This was constructed almost entirely in wood, to reduce weight, and to utilise labour and materials in the underused wood and furniture manufacturing industries.

The outbreak of war found DH with little Air Ministry work, so in September 1939 the firm proposed a fast twin-engined unarmed bomber called the DH.98, where speed and performance would not be affected by defensive turrets and other excrescences, which added weight and spoilt the design's clean aerodynamic lines. This aircraft would also have an outstanding performance such that little defensive equipment would be required, and it would employ DH's tried-and-tested methods of manufacture (wood or composite construction) used in its larger civil aircraft. The latter was especially suited to high speeds because all resulting surfaces would be smooth and free of rivets, overlapping plates and undulations.

The preliminary specification listed twin Rolls-Royce Merlin engines, a range of 1,500 miles, two 500lb or six 250lb bombs, two crew (pilot and navigator), and a maximum speed of 405mph at 20,000ft. On review, the Air Ministry considered 405mph to be very optimistic and eventually DH revised its figures to a more accurate 386mph at 20,000ft.

Official push-back

Within the Air Staff there was much opposition against the DH.98 project, one official document observing: "it is the definite view that, as a bomber for extensive use, [this] could not be so unless it carried effective rear defence. It is fully realised that this provision costs a certain drop in performance,

COMBAT
MACHINES

but the speed of opposing fighters and the conditions of operation are such that we cannot hope to depend upon obtaining security [just] by a margin of superior performance." Another added: "We have regretfully come to the conclusion that it would not be practicable to proceed with this type as a bomber." ACM Sir Edgar Ludlow-Hewitt, boss of RAF Bomber Command, was insistent on the absolute necessity of rear defence.

DH's unarmed bomber project was not, however, universally opposed. The Ministry's Sir Wilfrid Freeman and Sir Arthur Tedder were from the outset attracted by the proposal and gave great support. And neither the Air Staff nor Bomber

Command objected to producing an experimental high speed photographic reconnaissance aircraft, provided it was fitted with adequate rear defence. Accordingly, DH presented schemes for defensive armament, firstly similar to that used in the Handley Page Hampden (two guns each in upper and lower mid-fuselage positions) and then one with a tail turret and four guns. In each case DH stated frankly that the loss of speed would be substantial and fatal to the aircraft's purpose. Nevertheless, the latter design proved acceptable to the Air Staff and on January 22, 1940, an order was placed for two DH.98 Mosquito prototypes, Air Ministry representatives having examined ❯❯

The bright yellow Mosquito prototype wears Class B serial E0234 at a very wet and muddy Hatfield in November 1940. The undercarriage doors have not yet been fitted, while the orthochromatic film gives the impression the aeroplane is painted matt black, not yellow.
BAE Systems Heritage

This de Havilland view of E0234 at Hatfield on November 21, 1940 – during preparations for engine running – shows a more correct representation of its colour. The original short engine nacelles are evident and an Airspeed Oxford without propellers stands behind with, it appears, a Hurricane beyond that.
BAE Systems Heritage

Engine ground running of E0234 at Hatfield, taken on November 21, 1940, possibly just after the previous photo and of course prior to the maiden flight four days later. Phil Butler

E0234 is man-handled into position for engine ground runs on November 21, 1940. Landing gear doors are fitted. BAE Systems Heritage

a preliminary mock-up on December 29, 1939.

Note that contrary to many published sources, long before the outbreak of war the Air Ministry was well aware of the value of adopting wood for aircraft construction to save light alloys and forgings. And recent research by historian Ralph Pegram has shown that DH's concept for a fast unarmed bomber was not unique. During 1937-40 several firms – Airspeed, Armstrong Whitworth, Flight Refuelling, Folland, Handley Page and Short Brothers – submitted designs for high-speed bombers, some to be built in wood. Just how much DH knew of this rival work is unknown, but the story is described in Buttler's *British Secret Projects 4: Bombers 1935 to 1950* (Crécy 2020)

Eventually Freeman managed to get the defensive armament deleted from the prototypes (though examples with turrets were flown – see further on) and a draft requirement was raised for a High Speed Light Reconnaissance aircraft capable of 400mph at 18,000ft. The covering specification, B.1/40, was essentially written around DH's proposals. There was still fierce opposition inside the Ministry, however, and without Freeman's constant support the project could very likely have failed.

Once prototype flight testing had begun to show substantial promise in performance, a production order for 50 Mosquitos was placed. But for some time there was considerable confusion as to what versions would be built. The reasons behind this

situation were considerable and became quite involved.

Developments

De Havilland had always envisaged that a really fast design such as the DH.98 would have a variety of uses and, in May 1940, Sir Geoffrey de Havilland proposed an alternative long-range fighter to Wilfrid Freeman. By July 1940, increasing uneasiness about the unarmed bomber had caused interest to concentrate on this long-range fighter and that month the Minister himself authorised DH to construct the third prototype as a fighter (as the DH.98A). The covering specification F.21/40 described a two-seat, fixed-gun fighter with 4 × 20mm cannon and 4 × .303in machine guns all housed in the nose.

Concurrent with the Mosquito, the Air Ministry was in discussion with Airspeed over the delivery of a single-engined night-fighter called the AS.48. It soon became apparent that a variation of the Mosquito long-range fighter would suit this task better than the Airspeed proposal (at this time it was thought that a Mosquito night-fighter might require a nosewheel). Eventually, the long-range fighter was abandoned and work went ahead with the Mosquito night-fighter, based largely on the design with longer 'legs'.

DH promised that the 50-aircraft production order would be completed by July 1941. As an aid to the development and production process, a method of 'relaxed' control was adopted which, for example, would allow the first six aeroplanes to be built in the DH Experimental Department and inspected for workmanship only. In the end this idea of relaxed control with a mixture of production and hand methods proved unsuccessful (DH itself admitted as much) and brought some delay. Frustratingly, Mosquito production only started in July 1941 and remained a mere trickle for months, despite the order being increased from 50 to 200 at the start of that year.

This delay in production, however, came not just from the methods adopted. Also key were regular changes of design due to the evolution of the fighter requirements during late 1940-41 (based on combat experience), the failure of the Air Staff to decide if it definitely wanted the unarmed bomber version, and then what proportion of the total output would be built as fighters, bombers or reconnaissance aircraft. For example, after the prototype flew in November 1940 it was suddenly decided the unarmed bomber was no longer needed, and so the first aircraft scheduled as bombers were to be modified for photo-reconnaissance. The recce version, however, required much re-design of services such as the hydraulics and electrical fittings, which took more time.

At June 26, 1941, the Mosquito order book stood as follows: ⟫

Mosquito F.II night-fighter prototype W4052 was painted all-black to reflect its nocturnal role. The nose guns are just visible. These images were taken by an A&AEE cameraman on September 4, 1941, and would have been used primarily for recognition purposes. Crown copyright

E0234, later W4050, was the Mosquito unarmed bomber prototype and so sported a glazed nose. Photographed at Hatfield, the aircraft was built at Salisbury Hall. BAE Systems Heritage

W4050 with the longer nacelles, RAF colour scheme and a prototype 'P' symbol. Here the aircraft is being used as an apprentice training aid after it had been grounded.
Peter Green

1 Experimental prototype (unequipped)
1 Experimental night-fighter
1 Prototype photo-reconnaissance
2 Experimental turret fighters
19 Production photo-reconnaissance aircraft
27 Production night-fighters.

In addition DH then had orders for 150 night-fighters and 50 of a type yet to be specified. Then, shortly after this date, the firm was asked to convert, as rapidly as possible, the last ten production photo-recce aircraft back to bombers. Fortunately the bomber had not been cancelled.

This failure by the Air Ministry to provide final instructions as to exactly how many of each version were required proved a great handicap to both DH, and the Ministry of Aircraft Production (MAP – established in 1940 to co-ordinate the activities of Britain's aircraft industry and maximise the supply of aircraft to the armed forces). Full production of the Mosquito unarmed bomber was finally agreed on July 28, 1941.

Into the Air!
De Havilland had promised that its first prototype would be flying in nine months from go-ahead; this speedy construction was one of the firm's major claims for gaining an order. When the first prototype (essentially a flying shell) first flew at Hatfield in

November 1940 the manufacturer had exceeded its estimate by about two months. But this was in fact a very creditable achievement, when it is remembered that throughout the summer of 1940, with the Battle of Britain and other events ongoing, there had been universal dislocation to all types of experimental and development work.

When the first Mosquito prototype made its successful maiden flight on November 25, 1940, it carried class B mark E0234. Accompanying pilot Geoffrey de Havilland Jr as flight test observer was John Walker, the company's engine installation designer. Airborne trials moved forward swiftly, but wool tufts revealed that a stall was

Another well-known view of W4050 taken at Hatfield and showing the original nacelles. The Mosquito's clean lines still look impressive today... in 1940 they must have been a revelation. BAE Systems Heritage

occurring away from the rear nacelle, and was the most likely cause of some tail vibration. Indeed, at 240-250mph there was severe stalling along the rear inner portion of the nacelles. On a long journey this was fatiguing for a pilot, the symptoms exacerbating with stick movement fore and aft and a continual gentle up or down nodding of the nose.

The prototype, now wearing official military serial W4050, arrived at the Aeroplane & Armament Experimental Establishment (A&AEE), Boscombe Down, Wiltshire on February 19, 1941, for brief official handling and performance trials (though these ended five days later with a fuselage failure severe enough to require a full replacement). Nevertheless, 8 1/2 hours' flying had been logged, during which just gentle buffeting was experienced. No armament and operational equipment was installed, only specialist measuring apparatus, and the maximum weight was 16,800lb since problems with the fuel system meant the tanks could only be half filled.

Airframe W4050 was considered pleasant in the air, with generally good flying qualities. Aileron control was excellent, the elevators were rather heavy but effective and the rudder was also heavy. Take-offs and landings were straightforward and there was a considerable change of trim when the flaps were lowered. The aeroplane was unstable longitudinally on the climb, in level flight and on the glide, which was not serious but would be a handicap flying at night or on a long sortie.

Best recorded rate of climb was 2,880ft/min at 11,400ft, the estimated service ceiling approximately 34,000ft, and the maximum speed 388mph at 22,000ft. For many this last figure was a source of amazement. Officialdom had poured scorn on this possibility and no-one, not even DH itself, had been absolutely certain the 'Mossie' would be faster than the Spitfire. Yet here it was… 388mph! De Havilland designer

Richard Clarkson remembered Fred Rowarth of A&AEE taking his hat off to the Mosquito after completing the calculations. From then on the Mosquito was taken more seriously and early production machines would show an average maximum of 383mph. In fact previously, on January 16, 1941, Geoffrey de Havilland had flown the prototype alongside a Spitfire at 6,000ft with his father in the observer's seat. He was able to report that the new aircraft was able to fly away from the Spit in "a fairly convincing manner".

For the vibration problem, caused by the stall off the rear of the nacelles, RAE tunnel testing showed the ❯❯❯

It is thought that this view of W4052, in camouflage, was taken on April 19, 1942. The photo's reverse states it was one of the first images released to the public. Crown copyright

The mock-up Bristol four-gun turret fitted behind the cockpit of prototype W4050 and dated August 6, 1941. Unsurprisngly, this modification caused a substantial loss of speed through extra drag, although aircraft handling was fine. Note the missing wing skin. BAe Systems Heritage, Farnborough

Mosquito F.II DD723 fitted with Lancaster-type chin radiators in a Rolls-Royce photo, presumably taken at Hucknall in late 1943 or early '44. The nose radar appears to have been removed (or at least removed from the photo). Rolls-Royce Heritage Trust

W4050 on display at the first post-war SBAC Show, held at Radlett in September 1946. Particularly noticeable here are the three different sizes of drop tank on the ground alongside. Key Collection

most effective way to reduce this would be to extend the nacelle tail beyond the wing trailing edge. Subsequent flight tests with modified nacelles showed the tail buffet was almost gone, while the nacelle extension, along with a large fillet, reduced the model's overall drag to the point that the top speed rose by another 5mph. To check, on April 10, 1941, W4050 was flown with the original short nacelles and extremely severe tail buffet was experienced, but this was reduced markedly on the next flight after the long nacelles had been refitted. The first Mosquito prototype survived the war and today is preserved at the de Havilland Aircraft Museum at Salisbury Hall, Hertfordshire.

The recce prototype W4051 first flew on June 10, 1941, and its subsequent career is described later. The Mosquito F.II night-fighter prototype W4052 first became airborne on May 15, 1941 (the same day as Britain's first jet aircraft, the Gloster E.28/39). This flight was made directly from Salisbury Hall and on June 23 the aircraft went to A&AEE for trials. The resulting report described flights made at an all-up-weight of 18,395lb and, with the extended nacelles, the top speed was 376mph at 21,800ft. Another report, from February 1942, described

longitudinal stability tests where W4052 was fitted with two different tailplane sizes – respectively 88sq ft and 98 1/2sq ft in area. With the larger tailplane in place the stability was definitely improved, but not as much as expected. All three prototypes used Merlin XXI engines.

Turrets

Mosquito F.II serials W4053 and W4073 served as prototypes for trials with defensive turrets (all prototypes being built at Salisbury Hall). The original position to be assessed protruded into the middle of the bomb compartment, preventing bomb carriage. Moving the turret

as far aft towards the rear spar as possible made it likely that two 250lb bombs could be carried, but this move would mean the fuel tanks would have to be redesigned.

A dummy turret with four false guns was first flown on W4050 for aerodynamic trials on July 24, 1941, and it produced a serious loss in speed (although the aircraft's handing was satisfactory). With the guns aligned aft a speed of 352mph was recorded, and when facing sideways 334mph (both at 14,050ft). On September 14, 1941, W4053 flew with a turret, and W4073 first got airborne with one in place on December 5. However, another report stated that at 23,000ft the maximum full throttle level flight speed fell from 378 to 340mph with the turret, while on occasion the force from the slipstream onto the moving

turret prevented it from rotating. The idea of turret armament was finally rejected and W4053 and W4073 both became Mosquito T.III prototypes.

Deceleration

The signal quality of early air interception (AI) radars, such as the AI.IV 'arrowhead' set in the NF.II, left much to be desired. So the Mosquito's speed would be vital in catching a target, but would then present problems when approaching and manoeuvring to attack. The extra speed had to be discarded quickly enough to prevent an overshoot or collision, but late enough to ensure no loss of contact. It was recognised from the start that this would be difficult with the Mosquito's excellent aerodynamics.

In July 1941 de Havilland and RAE Farnborough agreed to a deceleration requirement of 250mph reduced to 180mph in just five seconds and tunnel tests of wing brake flaps, fuselage flaps and reverse thrust airscrews began in October. However, no suitable combination was found and the effort moved to fuselage brakes. These were test flown on W4052 between December 29, 1941 and August 1942. The first arrangement tried was a 'solid' dog-collar flap fitted beneath the fuselage only which was satisfactory up to 180mph, but buffet then began to develop. In mid-May W4052 ❯❯

AM. 11083.
FIG.2 NORMAL POSITION OF AIR BRAKES WHEN AEROPLANE IS STATIONARY. IN FLIGHT THE LOWER SET CLOSE

FIG.3. AIR BRAKES EXTENDED.

During the first half of 1942 fighter prototype W4052 was fitted with an experimental fuselage airbrake with 'battlement' type edges. Peter Green

The appearance of the final type of fuselage airbrake flight tested in July 1942. The view shows the airbrake position when W4052 was stationary; the lower set would close in flight. The venturi which operated the bellows is visible beneath the fuselage ahead of the airbrake. Crown Copyright

The same airbrake showing the fully extended position for flight. Crown Copyright

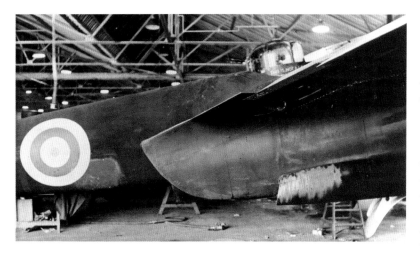

The Bristol B.XI four-gun turret fitted to one of the F.II 'turret prototypes' at Salisbury Hall, most likely W4053. Peter Green

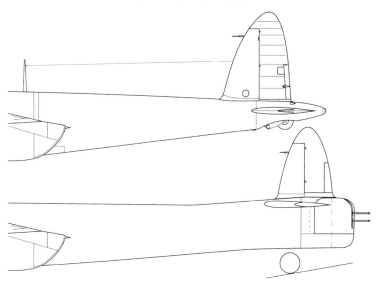

Prototype Mosquito W4050 still in use when pictured on September 2, 1942. Here it was fitted with Merlin 61 engines. Key Collection

A sketch produced from an original drawing observed in a 1945 cine film made by the de Havilland company to document the Mosquito's career; it is thought that the master drawing no longer survives. This shows the streamlined four-gun turret fitting (bottom) examined from mid-October 1939 for the Air Ministry; the wing and front half of the fuselage were believed to have been very similar to, or even identical to, the Mosquito itself. Andy Hay-Flying Art

tested a flap with 'battlement' edges, which encircled the fuselage like a cake frill. This was flight tested in various forms but by July results had shown that it was no better than dropping the undercarriage (which was another potential solution).

All fuselage brakes were operated by a venturi, which filled the bellows with air and, when flying at 250mph, took around three seconds to open fully. Each deceleration test was started by first throttling the engines and noting the decrease in speed with time with the brake closed, and then repeating the process with the brakes open. A&AEE reported that without applying the airbrake, W4052 took 45 seconds with the throttles closed to slow from 250mph to 150mph, and then 30 seconds with brake application. However, at high speeds with the latter there was pronounced elevator and rudder buffet and at 250mph the vibration was such that structural failure would eventually result. A&AEE concluded the air brake was unacceptable due to excessive buffet and insufficient retarding effect. In the end, dropping the undercarriage became standard practice for slowing the Mosquito night-fighter, though this never provided the speed reduction originally specified.

Chin radiators

In 1943 NF.II DD723 had chin radiators fitted in an attempt to

utilise standard 'power eggs'. During the middle war years the argument of bolting a common powerplant onto as many types of aeroplane as possible was seen as a useful step in helping production and maintenance. However, it is understood that there was never any intention of fitting 'power eggs' to Mosquitos and the DD723 trial was undertaken simply for comparison purposes.

DD723 was assigned to Rolls-Royce's test airfield at Hucknall, Nottinghamshire on July 26, 1943, to have Avro Lancaster-type power units fitted. In its original form DD723 had Merlin 23 engines which, in MS gear gave around 1,400hp for take-off and 1,480hp at its 5,500ft full-throttle height; in FS gear 1,420hp was available at 12,000ft (the Merlin 23 was used exclusively by the Mosquito and had a

two-speed supercharger).

Fitting two chin-type radiators involved removing the wing-type radiator/oil cooler units and fairing over the leading edges, reducing the wing area from 450sq ft to 441sq ft. The area of the new radiator ducts was modified to give the same degree of cooling as the original installation, Merlin 23s were retained and, for all flights before and after this refit, DD723 was flown at its operational weight with full armament and ammunition. No difference in speed was found between the two installations. Operating at 14lb boost in MS supercharger gear and 16lb in FS gear, the top speeds were 378mph at 14,900ft in FS and 360mph at 9,300ft in MS. The rate of climb for the underslung powerplants was "slightly inferior" to the standard form.

DD723's radiator trial flights occurred between November 3, 1943 and February 1, 1944, after which it went to de Havilland Hatfield with the underslung radiators still in place. A planned return to normal standard began in June 1944, but by December the NF.II was no longer in use operationally and, after December 11, DD723 never flew again.

MS and FS gear stand for Medium Supercharged and Fully Supercharged, relating to engine settings at different altitudes. Air gets thinner with height, so superchargers were introduced to piston engines to compress the air at higher altitudes to the equivalent pressure at sea level, or even more, thereby allowing the engine to produce the same levels of power at cruise altitude as it would at sea level.

These studies of DD723 were taken on February 11, 1944, soon after the aircraft had arrived at Hatfield. They are clearly posed with the propellers in near identical positions. BAe Systems Heritage, Farnborough

THROUGH THE LOOKING GLASS

This section explores the Mosquito's various glazed-nose bomber versions. To begin, however, there is a review of the aircraft's extraordinary structure, unique to British combat aircraft in World War Two

Mosquito B.IV DK338 captured in full fighting trim by an official cameraman.

The de Havilland Mosquito was a mid-wing monoplane built almost entirely in wood. Its one-piece wing displayed a small level of sweep-back on the leading edge and there was a sharply tapered trailing edge. Box spars were assembled using laminated spruce flanges and plywood webs, spruce and plywood compression ribs, and span-wise spruce stringers, and this was all covered with a plywood skin; the upper surface was in fact double and had further upper stringers sandwiched between the two skins. The leading edge was fixed to the front spar and built around nose rib formers and a D-shaped skin, while the wing structure was held together by glue, screws and pins and the plywood surface was then further covered by fabric. The cantilever tailplane was again made in wood with plywood-covered fixed surfaces and fabric-covering for the elevators and rudder.

Fascinating photo taken in April 1943 showing the assembly of one of the wooden sections of the Mosquito's structure. BAE Systems Heritage

Mosquito had an oval section monocoque fuselage constructed in jigs in vertical halves, each of which would have all of its equipment installed before the two sections were finally brought together. Bulkheads built from twin plywood skins – and kept separate using spruce blocks – carried the outer skin, which was a sandwich formed from a layer of balsa wood 7/16in thick and faced on both sides with 1.5mm-thick layers of plywood. The halves were scarfed together and, with the assembly complete, the entire fuselage was once more covered with fabric and doped. To permit the wing to be attached, the underside of the fuselage had to be cut away, but the lower portion of this removed section

was then re-attached once the wing had been fitted.

The bomb sight was situated in the nose forward of the pilot and navigator/wireless operator, who were seated side-by-side with the pilot on the left. The pilot was protected from behind by 7mm-thick armour plate from seat to head level and the navigator by 9mm-thick plating.

Two Rolls-Royce Merlin 12-cylinder Vee liquid-cooled engines were positioned on steel-tube mountings cantilevered from the centre wing spars, these driving 12ft-diameter de Havilland three-blade constant-speed full-feathering airscrews. Air was supplied by radiators positioned inboard of the engine nacelles ❯❯

A splendid air-to-air photo of Mosquito B.XVI ML963. Crown Copyright

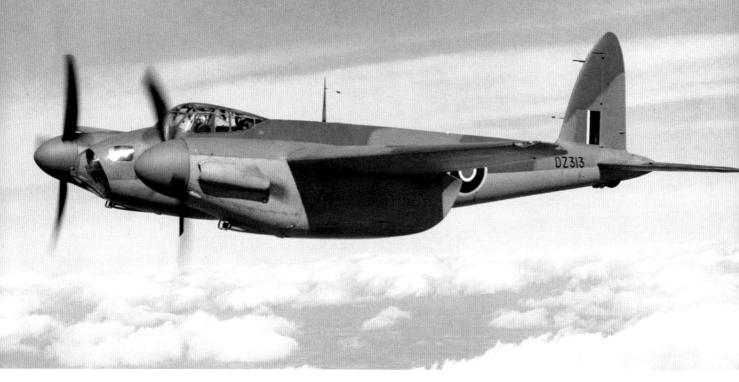

This image of B.IV DZ313 shows the propeller spinner neatly in line with the nacelle, typical of Mosquitos not fitted with high-altitude engines. BAE Systems Heritage

and housed within the wing thickness itself, with the inlets along the leading edge and the outlets (controlled by flaps) underneath the wing surface and forward of the front wing spar. To accommodate the radiators the wing leading edge between the fuselage and nacelles had been set 22 inches further forward.

Long 'legs'

The Mosquito B.IV bomber carried 118gal of fuel in four wing tanks outboard of the nacelles, another 289gal in four inboard wing tanks, and 136gal in two centre fuselage tanks between the wing spars, giving 543gal in ten tanks, all of which were

protected. A further 155gal could go in long-range fuselage tanks which, when fitted, extended the range from 1,400 miles to 1,800 miles. Long-range Mosquitos could also have two additional tanks (which could be jettisoned) mounted externally under the wing outboard of the nacelles, of various capacities.

Each unit of the hydraulically-operated retractable main undercarriage comprised two legs incorporating rubber-in-compression springing and carrying a single large wheel. These would retract into the rear of their engine nacelles to be enclosed by hinged doors; the wheel track was 16ft 4in. The Mosquito's relatively

light wooden airframe permitted the use of a small retractable tail wheel, which protruded slightly after being raised. The original 'Unarmed Bomber' Mosquito carried no guns but could take bombs both inside the fuselage and on racks underneath the outer wings. Initially the maximum internal load was two 500lb bombs, but cropping the stores' fins created enough space to carry four 500-pounders.

De Havilland's objective in choosing wood for the structure had been purely to simplify the production process itself and to make use of materials and labour, which were not required for the general aircraft programme. The firm claimed no special technical performance advantages through its use of wood over normal metal construction, and the resulting speed and performance came entirely from the design itself.

'Glass Nose' versions

Serial W4057 was the initial fully equipped Mosquito bomber prototype (though it had been converted from a photo-recce airframe) and as such it first flew in September 1941. The first production bomber was the B.IV, of which there were two forms. Series I airframes had short engine nacelles along with the early Merlin exhaust fitting, the run embracing serials W4064-4072. Although retaining the cameras, these aeroplanes carried four 250lb bombs and all had been

Internal detail of the Mosquito cockpit with its myriad dials and switches. Key Collection

completed by February 1942.

The full production standard B.IV, known as the Series II, introduced 1,460hp Merlin 21s with shrouded engine exhausts and longer nacelles; late-production machines were powered by the Merlin 23. This was the first iteration to carry the four 500lb bomb load internally and a 50gal drop tank could go under each wing (gross weight with bombs and tanks = 20,670lb). Some early Series IIs retained the original camera ports ahead of the bomb bay doors and in the rear fuselage; Hatfield constructed 292 examples.

The B.IV entered service in late 1942 and was subsequently further adapted to take a 4,000lb Blockbuster bomb internally (also known as a 'Cookie', this was a blast bomb with 75% of its weight formed of explosives, enclosed in a thin-casing). Carrying this required new bulged bomb-bay doors and the first conversion (DK594) began in November 1943.

Quite a number of B.IVs were modified to take 'Highball' bouncing bombs recessed in the weapon bay

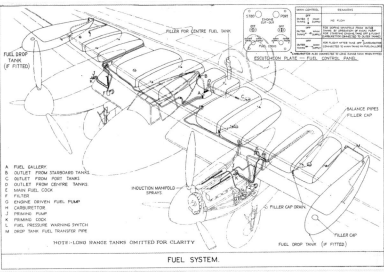

Original de Havilland drawings showing the Mosquito's fuselage construction.

to attack ships (essentially, a smaller version of the remarkable bouncing bomb first designed by Barnes Wallis to destroy dams), there was also a Pathfinder Mk.IV and a few examples were equipped for meteorological work. The B.IV's maximum speed was given as 380mph at 17,000ft and its ceiling 34,000ft.

One early Mosquito was converted to the experimental B.V with a stronger 'Standard' wing designed to carry 50gal drop tanks or 500lb bombs, but this mark did not reach production. Next on the list was the B.VII, based on the B.V and built specifically by de Havilland Canada at Downsview, Ontario. Powered by 1,460hp Packard Merlin 31 or 33 engines, 25 were built with the first example (serial KB300) flying for the first time from Toronto on September 24, 1942.

The B.IX high-altitude unarmed bomber was based on the reconnaissance PR.IX version and ➠➠

A 4,000lb 'Cookie' blast bomb is rolled underneath a Mosquito's fuselage ready to be lifted up into its bomb bay.
Key Collection

The enlarged bomb bay doors for the 4,000lb Cookie bomb can be seen clearly on this Mosquito, which is almost certainly B.XVI ML963.
Crown Copyright

had special 1,680hp Merlin 72s to enable it to operate at high altitude for prolonged periods. These aircraft had longer nacelles and introduced an air intake for a new reverse-flow coolant system positioned underneath. They could carry up to four 500lb bombs in the bay plus two more under each wing and LR495 was the first of 54 B.IXs to be constructed, making its maiden flight on March 24, 1943. Some B.IXs were modified to take the large 4,000lb Cookie with the associated bulged bomb bay doors… once again a few operated in the weather reconnaissance role and some were fitted with Oboe or H2S electronic

Production line for Mosquito fuselage sections; RAF aircrew are inspecting the work.
De Havilland

equipment for Pathfinder duties. The B.IX's operational ceiling was recorded as 38,000ft.

Sweet sixteen

A development of the B.IX was the B.XVI which introduced a pressurised cabin to enable the bomber to perform operations at altitudes of up to 40,000ft, thus keeping them above the heights at which most enemy interceptors could operate. The first examples had Merlin 72 and 73 units installed, but the majority were powered by the Merlin 76 and 77 (the odd-number Mk.73 or Mk.77 drove a pump which provided the cockpit

pressurisation). Initial examples could carry a 3,000lb bomb load only, but eventually this mark had the bulged bay to enable the full 4,000lb load to be taken on board (this also required enlarged elevator balance weights).

B.IV airframe DZ540 was adapted to serve as the prototype B.XVI and as such first flew in July 1943. ML937 was the first B.XVI capable of carrying the 4,000lb bomb and it recorded its maiden flight on January 1, 1944. The equivalent Pathfinder B.XVIs received Oboe and selected aircraft had their glazed noses hidden underneath a coat of paint. Tail warning radar sets called Boozer and Monica were carried by these aircraft and the H2S set was in due course mounted within a radome positioned beneath the rear fuselage. The B.XVI was built at Hatfield and also by Percival Aircraft based at Luton, Bedfordshire, and in all more than 500 examples were produced.

The B.XX (or B.20 after the abandonment of Roman numerals) was based on the B.VII, it was built entirely at Downsview in Canada and introduced a higher percentage of American and Canadian fittings. The manufacturing run stretched to 245 machines with 80 powered by American Packard-built Merlin 31s and the remainder having Merlin 33s; apart from the first eight, all had provision to take drop tanks under the wings. The first two examples to be delivered, KB162 and KB328, arrived in the UK during August 1943. For service with the United States Army Air Force (USAAF), a total of 40

A photo taken at Hatfield on April 27, 1943, showing the rapid pace of Mosquito manufacture. De Havilland

B.XXs would have cameras installed to enable them to operate in the recce and meteorological roles. As such they were given the American-style designation F-8.

The B.XXIII/B.23 high-altitude development of the B.XX was not built; the intention was to fit this mark with the Merlin 69, should numbers of the Packard Merlin 225 run short. But the Packard remained in plentiful supply and instead, 400 B.25s were produced and fitted with Merlin 225s driving 'paddle' blades, of which just five had the bulged bomb bay. In the mid-1950s serial KA997, renumbered N1203V, was modified quite substantially to undertake high-altitude survey work for civilian organisations. The necessary alterations for this role included a new forward fuselage built in metal.

Mosquito B.25 KB669 pictured in April 1945. Crown Copyright

To conclude, the last Mosquito bomber version was the B.35, which was first flown on March 12, 1945. This too involved different versions (the bomber plus the PR.35 night reconnaissance aircraft and later the TT.35 target tug) and they would continue to serve for some time after the end of World War Two. The bomber was a further advance over the B.XVI with the main difference being the introduction of Merlin 113 and 114 engines in early production machines, or Merlin 113A and 114A later, driving 'paddle' propeller blades to give a top speed of 422mph. »

The glazed nose is shown to good effect in this frontal view of a B.IV. Crown Copyright

LR495 on June 9, 1943, and carrying smoke curtain installation (SCI) stores under its wings. This airframe was built at Hatfield in 1943 and served with A&AEE Boscombe Down. Crown Copyright

Bomb load was 2,000lb, all-up-weight 25,200lb and a pressurised cockpit afforded this version the ability to fly at heights to 42,000ft. The bulged bomb bay featured throughout and some examples again had the H2S radome underneath the rear fuselage.

In total, 273 Mk.35s were produced, mostly from Hatfield, but some 65 were manufactured by Airspeed at Southampton. After the war Spartan Air Services of Canada acquired a PR.35 plus another nine B.35s to fit them with a new 'blown' glazed nose, fuselage cameras both ahead of and to the rear of the bomb bay, wooden covers replacing the old bomb bay doors, and numerous other changes. This was done to enable them to perform extensive air survey work across Canada.

From 1952 slightly more than 100 B.35s were re-allocated as TT.35 target-tugs, which to begin with involved having a winch and a towed target installed internally; later an external winch was introduced underneath the Mosquito's forward fuselage. A few of these airframes were modified further into Met.35s for weather reconnaissance work.

All Mosquito bombers had a span of 54ft 2in and a wing area of 454sq ft. The length of the B.IV, B.VII and B.XX was 40ft 9 1/2in, the B.IX, B.XVI and B.25 were all 44ft 6in long, while the figure for the B.35 was 42ft 3in.

Flight assessments

The Air Fighting Development Unit (AFDU) tested early production B.IV W4065 at a weight of 19,400lb. This

Mosquito, powered by two 1,150hp Merlins, had joined the unit for its assessment on November, 12, 1941, and the text from the resulting report gives some idea of the early Mosquito's flying capabilities.

The Mosquito was considered highly manoeuvrable both when light and fully loaded. Its controls were light and positive at all speeds with the rudder rather heavier than the elevators and ailerons. Comparative trials were performed against a Spitfire Mk.Vb, in which both aircraft carried full operational loads (W4065 had a full load of fuel and 1,000lb of bombs throughout, though very little difference was noticed in flight after the bombs had been removed). At 21,000ft altitude, and without emergency boost, the

On April 9, 1943, B.IX LR495 was photographed with bombs attached to pylons underneath its wings. Crown Copyright

The modified nacelle for Merlins designed for high altitude flying, which had an additional air intake for the reverse-flow coolant system placed underneath. BAE Systems Heritage

Mosquito appeared 4-5mph faster than the Spitfire, which had to use emergency boost to keep up. This gave the Mosquito a true top speed of around 375mph. At 600ft both aircraft attained approximately the same speed but the 'Spit' again had to employ emergency boost when the Mosquito did not. Above 24,000ft the performance of W4065 appeared to fall away in comparison to the Spitfire.

In addition, the bomber could climb quickly, especially when in unladen condition, and at its maximum rate of climb it could reach 20,000ft in just over nine minutes from the start of the take-off run, only about 2 1/2 minutes longer than the time taken by the Spitfire. Adding the bomb load did not seriously degrade the bomber's climb performance and the operational ceiling appeared to be about 30,000ft.

It was found that when flying at fast cruise, the loss in speed caused by the opening of the Mosquito's bomb doors brought a reduction of around 20mph after approximately three minutes' flying. The doors would open in 13 seconds and close in 11 seconds and the time taken to accelerate back to the original speed was approximately 30 seconds from the commencement of door closing.

When diving, the Mosquito accelerated well and in a slight dive at altitude it would reach the limiting speed of 360mph Indicated quite quickly. Single-engine flying was performed with each engine feathered in turn and the 'Mossie' could maintain its height and climb comfortably on one engine. The 1,000lb bomb load

appeared to make very little difference to the single-engined handling, turns with and against the live engine being performed with considerable ease.

If the Mosquito was cruising fast, the only present-day fighters likely to be a threat against it would have to dive down from a greater height than the Mosquito to attain enough speed to prosecute an attack. Fighters climbing from below would never come within

range, and any flying on the same level as the Mosquito, if spotted in time, could be kept out of range if the Mosquito accelerated quickly.

Nocturnal performer

No difficulty was experienced in night flying, the lighting being good for all essential instruments and cockpit controls without causing reflections on to the cockpit hood. The exhaust **»**

TA638 was an example of the final bomber Mosquito mark, the B.35. All of this series were built with larger bomb bay doors. Crown Copyright

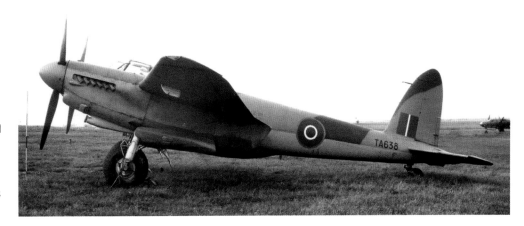

B.XVI ML959 poses for the official cameraman in February 1944. Crown Copyright

Air-to-air views of Mosquitos were taken by Boscombe Down from all angles to provide reference images for recognition purposes. Unfortunately, the identity of this B.XVI cannot be determined.
Crown Copyright

flames, however, which could not be seen from the cockpit, were rather bright when viewed from behind (as noted, shrouded engine exhausts were introduced on B.IV Series II aircraft).

As the Mosquito was superior in speed to the Spitfire Mk.Vb at all heights up to 24,000ft, the bomber's best evasion tactic was to accelerate away and prevent the fighter from coming into range. However, if the Spitfire attacked with a 3,000ft advantage, the Mosquito was never able to accelerate enough from fast cruising to prevent the 'Spit' from diving down below and getting in a burst of fire from astern of fairly long duration. But if the Spitfire was only about 2,000ft above and 1,000 yards away on the beam, the Mosquito could escape.

In each case the latter's acceleration was helped by the aircraft going into a slight dive. In due course it was found that a corkscrew manoeuvre, though difficult to perform at height in W4065, would do much to upset the fighter's aim, especially at long range.

The crew's external view was good, save backwards and downwards where it was poor and which meant fighters could approach from the rear without the Mosquito crew being aware of their attacks. This was not helped by having both crew facing forwards, but mirrors fitted in blisters would help to reduce this problem. It was found that wide weaving in flight was necessary to keep the blind spots in view as much as possible, but it proved very difficult even with relatively wide weaving to

spot a single fighter flying at more than 1,000ft below .

With the Mosquito's forward view being extremely good, low flying could be carried out quite easily, and with practice fairly steep turns and evasions were possible at high speed. W4065 was fitted with the standard Marconi radio installation for bombers, which had proved satisfactory and the intercommunication between pilot and navigator was considered very good.

A&AEE Boscombe Down also made its share of Mosquito assessments and the establishment's reports provide further detail of the bomber versions' splendid performance. Canadian-built B.XX KB328 was tested during the autumn of 1943 and gave a maximum rate of climb in MS gear of 1,780ft/

Target tug TT.35 prototype RS719, adapted from the B.35 and fitted with a wind-driven winch, wire guide and guards to the tailwheel and tailplanes.
Crown Copyright

min up to 10,000ft and in FS gear 1,440ft/min at 16,600ft; its service ceiling was 29,700ft and absolute ceiling 30,600ft. Having taken off at a weight of 21,430lb (with a 2,000lb bomb load) the maximum speed was 354mph at 7,000ft in MS gear and 364mph at 12,500ft in FS gear.

During the same period B.IX LR495 was tested at 22,850lb weight, including carrying 500lb bombs externally on faired racks under the wings, and the maximum speed in MS gear was 375mph at 10,600ft and for FS gear 388mph at 23,000ft, both with 21lb of boost. Maximum rate of climb (MS) was 1,830ft/min at 14,000ft and (FS) 1,080ft/min up to 26,700ft, service ceiling 35,200ft and absolute ceiling 36,000ft. LR495 had also been tested in May 1943 without external bombs aboard and the figures recorded were MS gear 393mph at 13,800ft and 2,060ft/min at 14,000ft, FS 405mph at 25,700ft and 1,310ft/min up to 26,700ft, service ceiling 37,000ft, absolute ceiling 37,800ft.

Author's note: sources vary considerably as to the weight and performance data given for different marks of Mosquito.

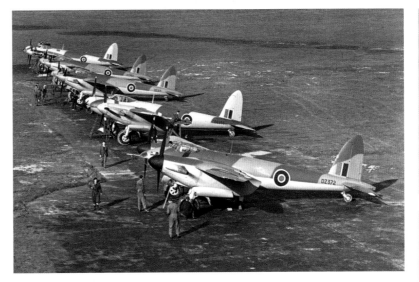

W4065 taken on December 29, 1941 at RAF Wittering, during its assessment with the Air Fighting Development Unit. The photo was made just two weeks after the AFDU had moved from Northolt to Duxford.

A wonderful mix of bomber (DZ372 nearest, DZ371 and DZ362) and fighter Mosquitos (DZ253 second nearest and DZ255) parked at Hatfield on November 2, 1942. Note the different camouflage. BAE Systems Heritage, Farnborough

This superb underside study of a B.IV was taken on August 28, 1943, by an A&AEE Boscombe Down photographer. The bomb doors, and the radiator outlets underneath the inboard wing surface, are evident. Crown Copyright

SENIOR SERVICE 'MOSSIE'

Just one Royal Navy Fleet Air Arm (FAA) frontline squadon operated what became the Sea Mosquito… though numerous training and support units acquired their own examples

I n early 1944 all Royal Navy carrier-borne squadrons were equipped exclusively with single-engine aircraft, but it was apparent that future operations might require something with rather more range and/or warload. Consequently, deck trials were performed using a Mosquito FB.VI, a type considered representative of modern high-performance twin-engined aeroplanes and offering great increases in range over current types, along with high performance.

On March 25, A&AEE test pilot Lt Cdr Eric 'Winkle' Brown landed LR359 (modified with a Fairey Barracuda A-frame-type arrester hook attached to the underside of a strengthened rear fuselage) on the deck of HMS *Indefatigable*, the first occasion that a twin-engined aircraft had landed aboard a carrier.

On June 12, 1945, LR387 was used to demonstrate the labour-intensive nature of manually folding a Sea Mosquito's wings. Due to cost, the Sea Mosquito was never provided with enough hydraulic power to enable folding to be operated from the cockpit.
BAe Systems Heritage, Farnborough

The first deck landing of a twin-engined aircraft... Lt Cdr Eric Brown lands Sea Mosquito LR359 onto HMS *Indefatigable*. Note the unenviable position of the 'batman' (deck landing officer) who for this trial had to stand near the deck centreline because the Merlin engines were blocking the pilot's view to one side (where the 'batman' would normally be standing). Crown Copyright

The TR.37 prototype TW240 displays this mark's much larger nose radome in a photo taken in November 1946. Crown Copyright

Two Merlins, with propellers rotating in the same direction, would create swing due to torque, which could make the Mosquito difficult to keep straight on a deck. So, to prevent it from hitting the carrier island, it was landed with the starboard engine rather than the nose above the deck centre line (as was usually the case). Seven satisfactory landings and take-offs were completed and further trials took place with *Indefatigable* on May 9-10, 1944. Take-offs were made at weights from 16,000lb to 22,000lb but landings were held to 20,000lb due to the arrester wire limits.

The pilots experienced no difficulties with landing aboard ship but, because the Mosquito's closing speed was higher, the radius of the approach circuit was greater than for current naval types and the final approach further back. At 16,000lb weight, the speed during the first part of the approach was 105mph with touch-down at 85mph; for 20,000lb it was 115mph and 98mph.

The take-off run was short but the problem of swing prevented full power from being used. Engines were synchronised for take-off and when the brakes were released and full throttle applied (with 8lb boost), full rudder was required for just two seconds to overcome any swing. Only well-trained pilots were allowed to fly Mosquitos from flight decks (fitting handed engines would have avoided swing altogether, but it never happened) and in the end the Sea Mosquito was never embarked in squadron service; however, the trials were useful for the forthcoming DH Sea Hornet.

New versions

A Naval Staff memo of August 27, 1944, noted that the only ships then able to operate Mosquitos ❱❱

Mosquito FB.VI LR359 was chosen for modification as a partial Sea Mosquito prototype for the Royal Navy. It is seen here as converted with the arrestor hook just visible and a 'P' Prototype mark on the fuselage... and no wing fold. Martin Derry

A splendid air-to-air photo of production TR.33 TW256 953/LP of 771 Squadron taken on October 27, 1947. 771 NAS operated from RNAS Ford as a Fleet Requirements Unit for training.

First production TT.39 target tug PF606 seen on September 23, 1948. This was one of the Mosquitos converted into a Sea Mosquito with, among other items, the extended and unflattering glazed nose.
Crown Copyright via Jeremy Collins

were *Indefatigable* and *Implacable*, with 24 plus 24 fighters each, or 30 Mosquitos only. Specification N.15/44 covered what became the Torpedo/ Reconnaissance TR.33 (based on the FB.VI). The A-frame arrester hook had a bulkhead in the fuselage above the attachment points, and 1,620hp Merlin 25s drove 12ft 6in-diameter propellers.

LR359 was a partially navalised conversion, which retained its fixed wings, but the second prototype LR387 had manually folding wings outboard of the flaps. Similar to Hornet, Alclad sheet was inside the top and bottom wing surfaces for extra strength, both inboard and outboard of the folding joint. Folding the wings was difficult and required several people using a pole, but a complete redesign of the hydraulics would have cost time and weight (the rise from wing folding itself was just over 300lb). With wings folded TR.33's span was 27ft 3in and height 13ft 6in.

During a carrier touchdown FB.VI's rubber-in-compression main

undercarriage made the aircraft bounce, so a pneumatic undercarriage was fitted to the 14th production TR.33 onwards; later Sea Mosquitos also had smaller wheels (as used on the Beaufighter). The four nose cannon were retained but the machine-guns were replaced by an American anti-shipping radar in a thimble radome. Two 500lb bombs could be loaded internally with one more under each wing; two 50gal drop tanks, or two 30gal tanks and two rockets, were alternative wing loads. New under-fuselage loads were an 18in torpedo (single-point attachment with steadying points fore and aft - when carried the bomb doors were closed and bomb bay empty), a 2,000lb bomb or an anti-shipping mine. Provision was made on the rear fuselage for rocket-assisted take-off gear, which could be jettisoned.

Varying tasks

Thanks to its diverse duties the Mk.33's performance was considered an all-round compromise. Two development

TR.33s built at DH Leavesden were TS444 and TS449 and 50 production aircraft followed. On September 15, 1945, 811 Naval Air Squadron reformed with a batch of 15 FB.VIs, and then TR.33s arrived from April 1946. This unit, the only frontline Sea Mosquito squadron, disbanded in July 1947. TR.33s TW228 and TW230 were used in post-war 'Highball' bouncing bomb trials as the only Sea Mosquitos allocated to an RAF unit, the Highball Trials Flight at Coningsby, which existed from January 1946 to November 1947. 751 NAS flew the FAA's last TR.33s until June 1953.

Next came the TR.37 with a British ASV.13B radar inside a larger 'bull-nose' radome and modified front fuselage. TR.33 TW240 acted as the prototype and 14 more were constructed by DH Chester, the last serving until May 1950.

The final Sea Mosquito was the inelegant TT.39 target tug and gunnery target, two prototypes and 24 production being converted from B.XVIs by General Aircraft at Hanworth against Specification Q.19/45. This introduced an extended and upward curved glazed nose for a camera operator (overall length 43ft 4in) and a glazed dorsal cupola for the winch operator, taking the crew to four. The propeller diameter was reduced to accommodate the wider nose, and Merlin 72/73s gave a towing speed of 300mph. TT.39 could also be used to calibrate ground-based radars, but the changes spoilt its flying characteristics and the stalling speed rose by 11mph. It flew with Fleet Requirements Units (FRUs) both in the UK and Malta.

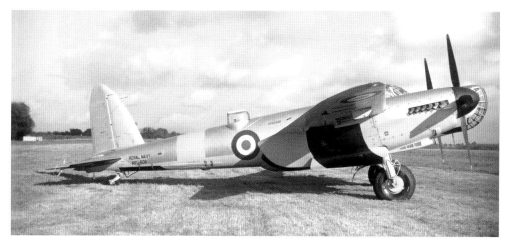

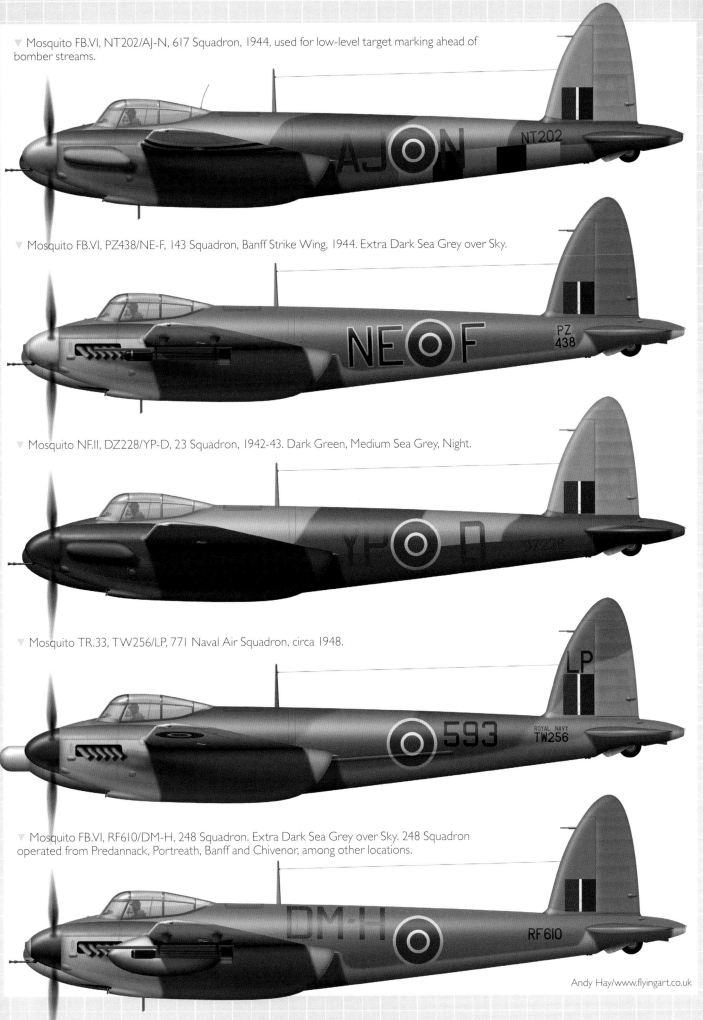

▼ Mosquito FB.VI, NT202/AJ-N, 617 Squadron, 1944, used for low-level target marking ahead of bomber streams.

▼ Mosquito FB.VI, PZ438/NE-F, 143 Squadron, Banff Strike Wing, 1944. Extra Dark Sea Grey over Sky.

▼ Mosquito NF.II, DZ228/YP-D, 23 Squadron, 1942-43. Dark Green, Medium Sea Grey, Night.

▼ Mosquito TR.33, TW256/LP, 771 Naval Air Squadron, circa 1948.

▼ Mosquito FB.VI, RF610/DM-H, 248 Squadron. Extra Dark Sea Grey over Sky. 248 Squadron operated from Predannack, Portreath, Banff and Chivenor, among other locations.

Andy Hay/www.flyingart.co.uk

SPITTING FIRE

This Mosquito
carries rockets under
the outer wings.
Crown Copyright

This section looks at the 'gun nose' fighter, fighter-bomber and intruder Mosquito marks plus specialised types based on or modified from these airframes. It cannot be stressed enough just how incredibly versatile the Mosquito was. Here, the night-fighter versions received successively improved marks of radar and the fighter-bombers carried different types of external tanks to provide longer range and maximum combat performance. Bomber marks covered earlier introduced highly specialised radar to enable them to unload their stores very accurately.

The offensive power of all versions was also improved in equal measure. The fighter-bomber's normal armament of four .303in Browning machine guns and four 20mm cannon was supplemented by eight rocket projectiles carried under the outer wings, and these aircraft were also adapted to carry bomb loads of up to 2,000lb. In addition, the Mosquito airframe was ideal for conversions to perform certain specialised functions, for example as a civil transport for certain routes crossing enemy occupied territory, as a dual-control trainer, and then as the famous 'Tsetse' ship and U-boat buster, which had a

6-pdr gun installed underneath the nose… a huge weapon for such a modest-size aeroplane.

Creating the Fighter

The fighter Mosquito was first proposed by de Havilland as the DH.98A with two Merlin XX engines, four machine guns and four cannon, and an extended fin. Its span was 54ft 2in, length 40ft 6in and wing area 450sq ft, and when operating as a long-range fighter the estimated maximum weight was 18,076lb and as a home defence fighter 16,828lb. The estimated maximum speed was 395mph at 23,700ft.

As built, the fighter Mosquito did not sport the extended fin, but it did have the four Browning machine-guns mounted in a solid nose ahead of the armour bulkhead and four British Hispano cannon in the lower portion of the fuselage, which fired through apertures underneath the nose. Later, certain night-fighter marks would have some of the guns taken out to make room for more sophisticated radar scanners. Fighter-bomber Mosquitos had the same gun armament as the fighter, plus a bomb-bay which was equivalent to the rear half of the bay in the pure bomber. Here there was internal stowage for 1,000lb of bombs, while racks under the wings could take two more 500lb bombs, thus giving the maximum load of 2,000lb.

Night-Fighters

Nocturnal combat versions of the Mosquito would serve RAF Fighter Command from 1942 right through until 1955. As noted earlier, W4052 served as the prototype for the Mosquito Mk.II fighter version and it first flew in May 1941. All UK night-fighter Mosquito production was undertaken in de Havilland's own factories at Hatfield, Hawarden (Chester) and Leavesden.

The first production machines carried serials W4073 to W4099 and after February 1942, when role prefixes were adopted for UK military aircraft types, the Mosquito II was redesignated F.II, and then NF.II to cover the night-fighter role. NF.II had the AI.IV radar installed (AI for air interception), which featured an 'arrowhead' antenna in the nose, aerials both above and below the middle of the starboard wing, and dipole antennas close to the wingtips. The wing spar was strengthened, Merlin 21 or 23 engines were housed in long nacelles and the mark carried the full eight-gun armament, though flash eliminators had subsequently to be added to the machine guns to ensure the pilot was not blinded when they were used at night.

The first of the 494 F.IIs and NF.IIs manufactured was delivered in March 1942 and entered service in May; this total included 25 NF.II (Specials) fitted with Gee navigation to enable them to perform nocturnal intruder operations. These Specials would of course fly over enemy territory, so the AI.IV radar had to be taken out to ensure the enemy could not get his hands on this equipment via a downed Mosquito. Some examples (without any nose guns) had the Serrate radar-detector, used to home onto German night-fighter radar emissions, others with 100 Group had the AI.IV radar replaced with AI.V, and four were fitted with PR cameras. Finally, in 1942 six early NF.IIs were adapted into dual-control trainers, in advance of the arrival of the T.III trainer.

Based on the NF.II, the T.III crew conversion trainer introduced duplicate controls and was powered by either Merlin 21 or 23 engines. The turret fighter prototype W4053 was converted into the trainer prototype and as such made its maiden flight in January 1942. In all 368 T.IIIs were built.

The next night-fighter was to have been the NF.X with Merlin 61 ⟫

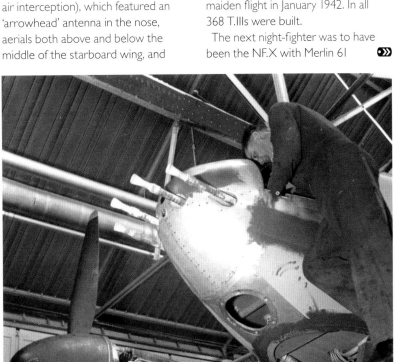

A Mosquito FB.VI pictured during maintenance work.

Mosquito FB.VI NT193 pictured in flight on April 26, 1944. Crown Copyright

powerplant but this mark did not enter production. Instead, the NF.XII was developed as a modified NF.II having an armament of just four cannon. More significantly, the more advanced AI.VIII 10cm wavelength radar was then introduced with its antenna housed in a 'thimble' nose radome (the machine-guns had to be taken out to make room). A total of 98 NF.IIs were upgraded to NF.XII standard by Marshalls of Cambridge,

still with Merlin 21 or 23 engines, and prototype DD715 first flew in NF.XII form in August 1942. Deliveries began in March 1943.

Next on the list came the NF.XIII developed from the FB.VI fighter bomber and powered by the Merlin 21 or 23 or (on late examples) the Merlin 25. This was a new-build NF.XII with AI.VIII radar, but the variant also featured the universal wing with the external fuel tanks developed for

the FB.VI. As before the radar was housed either in a thimble nose or in a universal or 'bull' nose and 270 were produced with the first (HK363) becoming airborne in August 1942.

The NF.XVII was a development of the NF.XII with Merlin 25s and an American radar housed in a bulbous nose, the SCR-720B which, in the UK, was designated AI.X. NF.II DZ659 served as the 'prototype' and 99 production machines followed, the

This early Mosquito T.III, HJ866, was photographed in September 1942. Tony Buttler Collection

first flying in March 1943.

A proposed development of the NF.XIII was to have been the NF.XIV with two-stage Merlin 67 or 72 power units, but this was not built and it was replaced in the development programme by the NF.XIX and NF.XXX. The NF.XIX was another NF.XIII development but powered by Merlin 25s with paddle-blade propellers and fitted with either the AI.VIII or AI.X radar in the usual thimble or universal nose. The return to AI.VIII was prompted by the poor supply of AI.X sets and with problems installing them in the Mosquito. The first NF.XIX flew in April 1944 and 280 were completed, with the mark entering service in May 1944.

The NF.XV was a high-altitude

Forward section of an FB.VI fighter-bomber. The bomb doors have been opened to provide access to the cannon. Tony Buttler Collection

A views taken by A&AEE Boscombe Down of NF.XIII HK428, which displays the different nose required for the AI.VIII radar. Crown Copyright

interceptor night-fighter based on the reconnaissance PR.VIII airframe and it carried the AI.VIII radar. This version had extended wingtips, which took the span to 62ft 6in and the wing area to 479sq ft (length 44ft 6in), Merlin 72/73s or Merlin 76/77s were fitted driving three or four-blade propellers and there was a pressurised cabin. When prototype MP469 first flew on August 8, 1942, it lacked its radar and the associated nose, and the usual four machine guns were still in place. When the radar was installed in this airframe the machine guns were moved to a new blister or pod attached underneath the fuselage. Despite ⟫

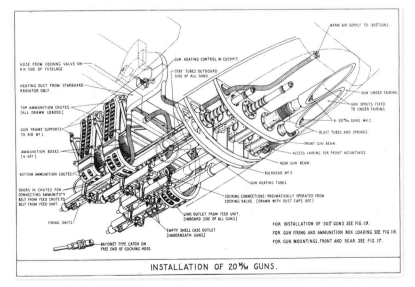

INSTALLATION OF 20 ᴹ/ᴍ GUNS.

The 20mm cannon installation fitted to fighter and fighter-bomber Mosquitos. Tony Buttler Collection

Early night-fighter W4076 pictured at A&AEE Boscombe Down on February 28, 1942. Note the aerials at each wing tip and those protruding above the centre starboard wing. Crown Copyright

The 20mm cannon barrels on an FB.VI. Key Collection

'paddle' propellers, along with deeper nacelles with an intercooler radiator on the underside and an extra chin intake in between the spinner and the carburettor intake. Dipole antennas positioned above and below the wingtips, with another offset on the fuselage port side, identified the AI.X/SCR-720 radar with its scanner housed inside a bulbous nose. The first of 529 NF.30s built appeared in April 1944 and deliveries began the following month.

A development of the NF.30 fitted with Packard-built Merlin 69s was to have become the NF.31, but this did not appear. The next series-built version proved to be the NF.36, another modified NF.30 which retained the AI.X and four 20mm cannon but had Merlin 113/114 or 113A/114A units. In all 163 were built and to begin with NF.30 airframe MT466 was refitted as a prototype. Production began in May 1945 with

having the capability to reach 43,000ft, just five NF.XVs were built, the other four having been converted from B.IV Series II airframes with the normal universal nose.

The NF.XXX/NF.30 was a high-altitude night-fighter development of the NF.XIX. Manufactured in the UK, it had two-stage Merlin 72, 76 or 113 engines driving three-blade

RK955 and the type joined RAF Fighter Command in January 1946. A few NF.36s were further modified for meteorological reconnaissance as the Met.36 version.

The NF.36 was further improved into the NF.38 powered by Merlin 114A engines, and this was the final night-fighter version to enter production. The planned radar was the AI.IXb but there were difficulties with this equipment and so many airframes actually received the AI.X. Three dipole antennas were positioned both above and beneath each wingtip and a key change was that the front windscreen was moved 5in further forward to provide extra space for the cockpit. NF.36 serial RL248 was converted into a prototype and altogether 101 were constructed. The rollout of the last of these aircraft, and indeed the last Mosquito to be manufactured, took place on November 15, 1950.

A line up of yellow Mosquito T.IIIs, post war, with VT613 nearest. BAE Systems Heritage

Fighter-Bomber and Intruder

The first fighter-bomber Mosquito version was the FB.VI in both Series I and Series II form and developed from the NF.II night-fighter. HJ662/G (formerly DZ434) served as a prototype and flew for the first time on June 1, 1942, the first production machine flew in February 1943 and the type entered service in the spring of 1943. The FB.VI retained the NF.II's nose gun armament with Series I machines having Merlin 21 or 23 engines and Series II the Merlin 25.

This type had the strengthened universal wing, which permitted two 500lb bombs, eight 60lb rocket projectiles or two 50gal drop tanks to be carried (single-tier underwing rocket launchers were subsequently replaced by two-tier launchers). The capability of carrying eight 60lb rocket projectiles (four per wing) was introduced in 1944, although after service entry the 60lb was subsequently replaced by the 25lb rocket. Series I machines could have two 250lb bombs loaded into the rear of their bomb bays (the forward portion of the bay housed the ⟫

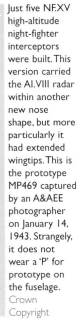

Just five NF.XV high-altitude night-fighter interceptors were built. This version carried the AI.VIII radar within another new nose shape, but more particularly it had extended wingtips. This is the prototype MP469 captured by an A&AEE photographer on January 14, 1943. Strangely, it does not wear a 'P' for prototype on the fuselage. Crown Copyright

Nose view of a Mosquito NF.19. Crown Copyright

Spectacular post-war photo of T.III TV959 taken in flight prior to delivery. The view provides excellent underside detail for the Mosquito's airframe. Built at Leavesden, this aircraft has training ID bands around the middle wings and its rear fuselage. Tony Buttler Collection

cannon breeches) but the Series II was able to take two 500lb internally.

Some FB.VIs also carried an AI.IV radar, while a few more had the capability to carry the AI.XV air-to-surface radar within a cylindrical body fitted on the nose, which enabled

these machines to perform low-level night-fighter operations. Once again several were fitted for use as meteorological reconnaissance aircraft and nine more had all of their armament removed to enable the British Overseas Airways Corporation

(BOAC) airline to use them as courier aeroplanes. In all, almost 2,300 FB.VIs were constructed with 57 coming from Airspeed at Christchurch, 1,066 from Standard Motors at Coventry and the rest from de Havilland.

The next fighter-bomber Mosquito mark, though produced in small numbers, is one of the most well-known and impressive versions of the aircraft. The FB.XVIII anti-ship and anti-tank variant was based on the FB.VI but had a six-pounder 57mm quick-firing cannon (with Molins auto-loader) replacing the four 20mm within the lower nose, but retaining the four machine-guns. This Mosquito was nicknamed 'Tsetse', after the large biting fly that inhabits tropical Africa, and examples carried the 'G' suffix on their fuselage serial numbers to ensure they stayed under permanent guard during periods on the ground. (During the war

With the bulbous nose required to house its AI.X radar, the NF.30 night-fighter was beginning to lose the balanced appearance associated so much with the Mosquito. Note the inlets beneath the propeller spinners on this example, RK953. Crown Copyright

'G' for Guard on UK military serial numbers was usually applied to secret prototypes such as the first jet aircraft, and to advanced or special versions of production types, such as Tsetse.)

The six-pounder's barrel would protrude from beneath the aircraft's nose section, the gun itself weighed 1,580lb and 24 rounds could be carried. To save weight the number of machine guns was soon cut back to just two. Prototype HJ732/G made its maiden flight on June 8, 1943, and 19 'Tsetses' were manufactured, each of them powered by Merlin 25 engines.

Neither the Merlin 72-powered FB.X or the FB.XI powered by Merlin

Official Ministry photo of Mosquito FB.VI fighter-bomber HJ719 taken in May 1943. Crown Copyright

NF.36 night-fighter RL248 was converted to act as the Mosquito NF.38 prototype. This shot was taken after the modifications had been completed in January 1947. Crown Copyright

61s were built and just three FB.21s (based on the FB.VI) were completed, all at Ontario, before Canadian production moved to the later FB.26. The T.22 was a dual-control trainer built in Canada, it was a development of the FB.21 powered by Packard Merlin 33s and six examples were produced. A further development of the FB.21 intended for manufacture by de Havilland Canada was to have been the FB.24 high-altitude fighter-bomber powered by Merlin 301 units, but this was cancelled before the two examples on order had been completed.

The next Canadian mark was the FB.26 fighter-bomber based on the FB.VI, which used single-stage Packard-manufactured Merlin 225 units, and the production run reached 335 machines in all. Next in the list came the T.27 dual-control trainer powered by Merlin 225s and based

on the T.22, with 49 in total built in Canada. The proposed FB.28 development of the FB.26 was not turned into hardware, while the 37 examples of the T.29 mark were all FB.26 fighter-bombers converted to dual-control trainers in Canada.

Fighter-bomber and trainer

Mosquitos were also built in quantity in Australia, by de Havilland Australia in a brand-new factory at Bankstown near Sydney and under the manufacturer's designation DHA.98. This effort resulted in four more Mosquito marks, and to help the firm a British-built NF.II, DD664, was despatched for ⟫

NF.II DD737 displays the black colour scheme worn by early Mosquito night-fighters, plus the wingtip and 'arrowhead' nose aerials for its AI.IV radar. Crown Copyright

An official recognition photo of Mosquito FB.VI serial NT193. Crown Copyright

use as a pattern aircraft. On arrival it was given the Australian serial number A52-1001.

The first Australian variant was the FB.40 fighter-bomber based once more on the FB.VI and manufactured primarily using Australian coachwood for the airframe. Coachwood, also known as scented satinwood or tarwood, produced a light timber, which could be worked

with ease. A total of 178 FB.40s were manufactured, the first 100 fitted with Packard Merlin 31 engines driving tapered-blade propellers and the remainder receiving Merlin 33s fitted with 'paddle' propellers. They also wore serials in the A52-series, signifying that these machines were for Royal Australian Air Force (RAAF) use only. The first example, A52-1, flew for the first time on July 23, 1943, though

the first delivery to the RAAF did not take place until March 1944. Problems with the glues used in manufacture brought further delay, but by the end of the war the de Havilland Australia production line was up to speed.

One production FB.40, serial A52-36, was later test flown with Packard Merlin 69s installed and, as such, was redesignated FB.42 and re-serialled A52-300. It was the only example so converted because this project was dropped, but the aircraft's performance at high altitude had been much improved by the new engines; in due course the FB.42 airframe was modified further to become the PR.41 reconnaissance prototype. Finally, between June 1944 and May 1947, 22 Merlin 33-powered FB.40s were converted to T.43 dual-control training aircraft, the modifications also involving the addition of dual elevator trim tabs.

In-Flight Assessment

Examples of night-fighter and fighter-bomber Mosquitos were tested thoroughly by A&AEE Boscombe Down throughout the war. NF.II W4076 underwent trials during April 1942 in a most unusual role. Tests made by de Havilland itself on F.II W4082 had shown that the top speed of the Mosquito when painted in a

FB.II W4087 was modified as the one-off Turbinlite Mosquito by Alan Muntz at Heston. This involved fitting a very powerful searchlight inside an extended nose to help locate enemy aircraft at night; the fitting had been completed by the end of 1941. The object was to illuminate the enemy so a companion aircraft could then shoot it down and 151 Squadron (from January 16, 1942), and then 85 Squadron (from February 18), test flew the installation. However, the concept was found to be flawed and was dropped. Key Collection

matt black finish (for the night-fighter role) was reduced by 26mph when compared with that obtained with a smooth black finish. However, similar tests made at Boscombe Down using W4076 showed that the matt black finish brought about a reduction in speed of just 8mph.

Performance tests of the Mosquito VI were required to cover the three versions – intruder, long-range fighter and escort fighter. In October 1942 prototype HJ662/G was used for handling and diving trials when loaded to represent the intruder version at an overload weight of 20,835lb. Boscombe's pilots found that the aeroplane was exceptionally manoeuvrable. Its controls were effective, well harmonised and reasonably light even in dives up to 425mph ASI, and if yaw was applied during the dive then wing drop would occur in the direction of the applied yaw.

The aeroplane was longitudinally and directionally stable under all conditions of flight, except firstly when on the glide with flaps and undercarriage down, when the Mosquito was neutrally stable longitudinally, and second when in level flight at low speed when there was a tendency to slight instability. Laterally the aeroplane was stable. If the speed was changed from the trimmed speed on the glide with flaps and undercarriage down, one wing would drop when the speed was increased, and the opposite wing would drop

with any decrease of speed.

In January 1944 FB.VI HX809 was used by A&AEE for level speed tests and figures of 353mph at 5,100ft and 354mph at sea level were recorded in MS gear, and then 363mph at 12,500ft and 369mph at 7,200ft in FS gear.

In April 1944, another FB.VI, HJ679, was used for bombing trials. Until that time, the dropping of underwing bombs from Mosquitos had been limited to a diving speed of 360mph ASI. This was because the bomb doors had to be opened before

the wing bombs could be released and 360mph was the limit for diving when the bomb doors were open. However, a modification had made it possible to drop the wing bombs without first opening the bomb doors. Consequently, it was desired to increase the limiting diving speed for underwing bomb loads to 450mph ASI. With this in view, diving trials to this higher speed were undertaken with HJ679 carrying various types of underwing bomb load to clear their release at this speed.

Excellent under-fuselage and engine nacelle detail is provided by FB.VI NS893, photographed prior to its receiving unit markings. Tony Buttler Collection

Former NF.II DZ659 photographed after modification to NF.XVII standard with a new nose and AI.X radar. At this time it was serving with the Fighter Interception Unit. Key Collection

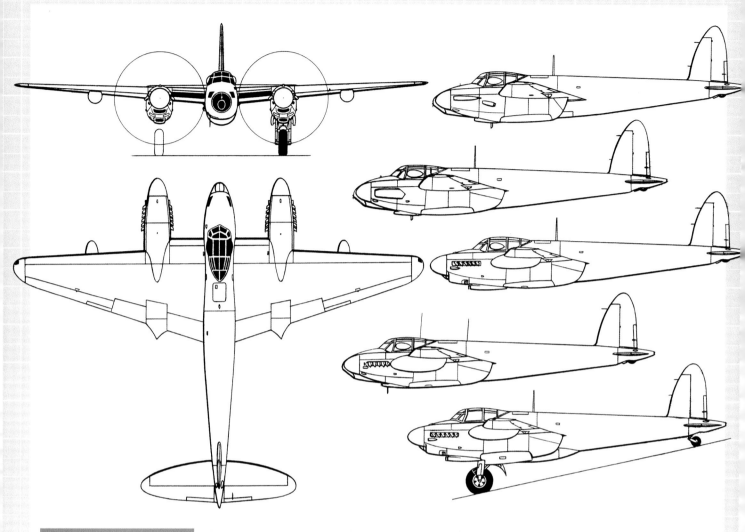

SPECIFICATIONS

Data for Mosquito B.XVI

Powerplant

Two 1,680hp Rolls-Royce Merlin
72/73 or 1,710hp Merlin 76/77

Dimensions

Span 54ft 2in

Length 44ft 6in

Wing area 454sq ft

All-up-weight

25,917lb

Performance

Maximum speed: 415mph at
28,000ft

Rate-of-climb: 2,800ft/min

Service ceiling: 37,000ft

Armament

One 4,000lb bomb in fuselage bay,
two 500lb bombs or eight rocket
projectiles under wings

The bomb aimer's position.
This unidentified Mosquito
has already completed 20
bombing missions.
Key Collection

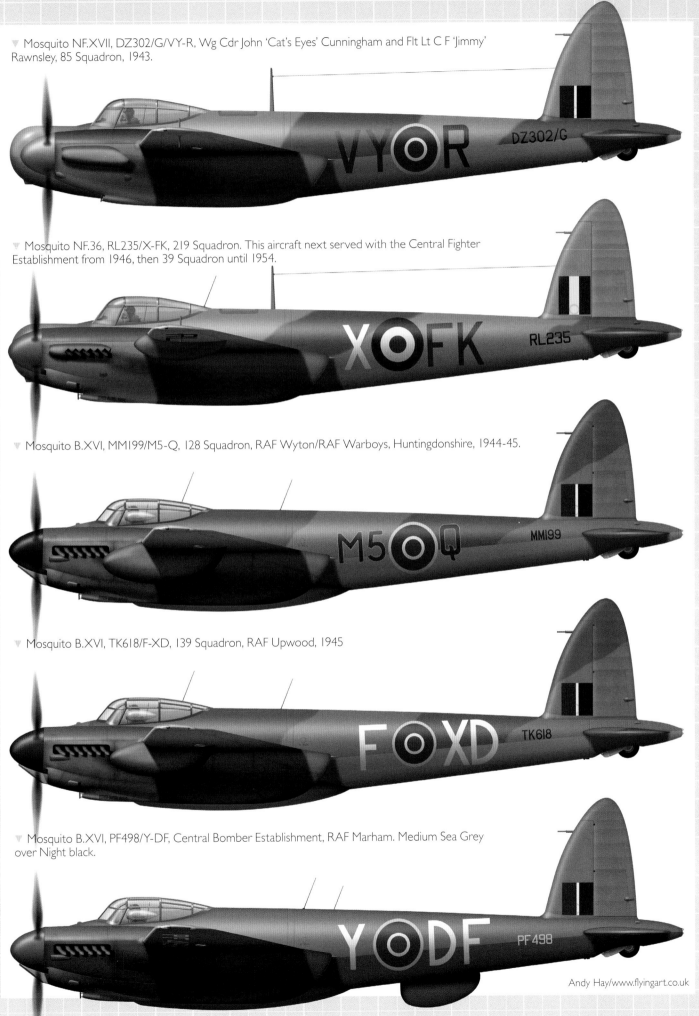

▼ Mosquito NF.XVII, DZ302/G/VY-R, Wg Cdr John 'Cat's Eyes' Cunningham and Flt Lt C F 'Jimmy' Rawnsley, 85 Squadron, 1943.

▼ Mosquito NF.36, RL235/X-FK, 219 Squadron. This aircraft next served with the Central Fighter Establishment from 1946, then 39 Squadron until 1954.

▼ Mosquito B.XVI, MM199/M5-Q, 128 Squadron, RAF Wyton/RAF Warboys, Huntingdonshire, 1944-45.

▼ Mosquito B.XVI, TK618/F-XD, 139 Squadron, RAF Upwood, 1945

▼ Mosquito B.XVI, PF498/Y-DF, Central Bomber Establishment, RAF Marham. Medium Sea Grey over Night black.

Andy Hay/www.flyingart.co.uk

n mid-November 1941, 105 Squadron became the first frontline RAF unit to receive the Mosquito bomber, although with production then not yet reaching full capacity, and fighter and reconnaissance versions required elsewhere, deliveries were initially slow (in January 1942 de Havilland's shadow factory at Leavesden flew its first Mosquito, so with Hatfield's own production the rate soon began to rise.) Early 105 machines were thus employed on crew training and it was not until May 31, 1942 that the Squadron's B.IVs made their combat début. Immediately following Bomber Command's first 1,000-bomber raid against Cologne on the night of 30-31, 105's aircraft flew individual nuisance bombing missions over the city during the day.

On September 19, 1942, after having assessed low- and high-level and shallow-dive forms of attack, 105 undertook the first high-altitude daylight raid of the war on Berlin, though just two Mosquitos reached the city. In November 1942, 139 Squadron became operational on the B.IV and from this point both units (operating within 2 Group) specialised in pin-point attacks against specific targets, primarily at low level; they went on to complete more than 100 successful daylight raids. The Mosquito's high performance was of great benefit, but the speed margin over the defending Focke-Wulf Fw 190s was not quite sufficient enough to ensure the attackers were always safe from interception and some were shot down.

On September 25, 1942, four B.IVs of 105 Squadron raided the Gestapo Headquarters in Oslo in Norway. Here, the Mosquitos successfully attacked in pairs at low level although one aircraft was lost to an Fw 190. Then, during the morning of January 31, 1943, 105 hit Berlin just when Chief of the German Armed Forces Hermann Goering was making a speech, and that afternoon 139 followed with a similar raid to disrupt

OVERLAND SERVICE

This section provides a general guide on the roles and tasks undertaken by RAF Mosquitos during the war and the theatres where the aircraft was active - apart from that is Coastal Command, covered in a later chapter. A brief review of rather quieter civilian activity closes this section

Some surplus B.35 Mosquitos were converted to TT.35 target tugs, and several would become the last active RAF examples, finally being retired in late 1963. Tony Buttler Collection

Cleared to fly: a pilot signs for his Mosquito from a member of the groundcrew in September 1944. Key Collection

Another night's work: This moody photograph shows Mosquitos taking off at dusk for their next operation. Rolls-Royce Heritage Trust

an address by Reich Minister of Propaganda, Joseph Goebbels.

On June 1, 1943, 2 Group became part of the Second Tactical Air Force (2TAF) and so 105 and 139 Squadrons moved to 8 Group, Bomber Command's Pathfinder Force (PFF), to begin one of the Mosquito's most vital roles… target marking for the main bomber force. This work required special navigation aids to help ensure the markers (usually flares) were dropped accurately over a target, the main force heavy bombers following to drop their loads on the markers. The first of these devices was called Oboe, a radar aid with which the Mosquito's navigator could track signals transmitted from two UK-based ground stations without having to refer to the ground below. Oboe would then tell him, with some accuracy, when his aircraft had reached its bombing point. Oboe's weakness was

its reliance on these ground stations, which limited operational radius.

B.IVs had also equipped 109 Squadron from mid-1942, but this unit was the first to receive the B.IX, in spring 1943, and its aircraft carried Oboe; 105 also had Oboe-equipped B.IXs and these two 8 Group PFF units began their specialised target-marking operations in December 1942, continuing in the role until war's end, by which time they had B.XVIs on strength (Oboe was first used by 109 Squadron for a raid on the Lutterade power station during the night of December 20-21,1942). Single Mosquitos, flying at up to 30,000ft and in darkness, were almost impossible to intercept and this work contributed enormously to the results obtained by Bomber Command during the second half of the conflict.

In the meantime, after joining 8 Group, 139 Squadron had from ⯈⯈

operational with H2S, a radar bombing system carried within the Mosquito that was entirely independent of ground stations, and therefore not limiting the operational radius. The arrival of H2S was a big step forward.

Light Night Striking Force

In April 1944, 627 was transferred to 5 Group as a marker squadron; sadly, it was on one of this unit's sorties, on September 19, 1944, that Wg Cdr Guy Gibson of Dam Buster fame died when his Mosquito crashed in Holland. In the meantime, 139 and 692 Squadrons, both within 8 Group, had formed what would became a powerful and most successful body within Bomber Command, the Light Night Striking Force (LNSF), something of an outgrowth of the Pathfinder Force. It was 692 that dropped the first 4,000lb 'Cookie' bomb from a Mosquito, over Düsseldorf on February 23-24 (which was in fact the first raid entirely comprising Mosquitos). By this time 139 had the B.XVI in service.

Further additions to the LNSF included 128, 571, 142, 162 and 608 Squadrons and, right through until the end of the war, the LNSF operated over Germany to hit targets with admirable precision. With its 4,000lb

In mid-January 1943 *Aeroplane* magazine reported on a visit to a Mosquito unit's base. In fact this was 105 Squadron, the first frontline RAF unit to equip with the new aircraft, and these photos were taken during that publicity visit.
Key Collection

October 1943 a new role flying 'spoof' nuisance raids. Here, the primary objective was not to inflict damage (though bombs were taken) but rather to divert the enemy's attention from targets being raided by the heavy bombers, to cause general disruption within Germany's defences, and to halt the manufacture of war materials by triggering air raid alerts,

all with minimum use of aircraft. The Squadron's B.IXs carried G-H, another radar aid (which did require position plotting inside the aircraft itself) and they would often use 'window'… a countermeasure created by dropping a cloud of thin strips of aluminium to block or saturate German radars (today known as chaff). Then in January 1944, 139's B.IVs became

bomb and auxiliary fuel tanks, the high-altitude B.XVI proved perfect for such sorties and Berlin became the Mosquitos' favourite target. During March 1945 the city was attacked on 27 consecutive nights, with all LNSF squadrons taking part on March 21-22.

The final production bomber version was the B.35, which was not operational during the war, but afterwards it served in Bomber Command with 109 and 139 Squadrons and in Germany with 14 and 98 Squadrons. The Mosquito was also in Germany post-war with 4, 11, 21, 69 (renumbered from 613 in August 1945) and 107 squadrons. In addition, 146 surplus B.35 bombers were converted to TT.35 target tugs and some of these became the last RAF Mosquitos to serve in the UK, in the hands of 3/4 Civilian Anti-Aircraft Co-operation Unit at Exeter; this unit finally relinquished its aircraft in May 1963. Another 15 B.35s were converted for night flash photography as PR.35s.

Night-Fighters and Fighter-Bombers

The first fighter Mosquitos were initially concentrated in the UK and by July 1943, 11 squadrons were on strength with nine assigned to night defence duties. The first to convert were 151 and 157 and it fell to the former to claim the first confirmed kill, in late June 1942. However, the early AI.IV radar in the NF.II was soon made obsolete by AI.VIII centimetric radar (with a wavelength of 10cm rather than the 1.5 metres of the AI.IV). This enabled much smaller objects to be detected and required smaller antennas than the earlier, lower frequency sets. Consequently,

AI.VIII gave a more straightforward installation with the scanning dish reflector and the aerials all grouped together in the nose, and a vastly superior performance when tracking enemy aircraft. The result was the Mosquito NF.XII and the quality of the equipment it carried meant this version was not permitted to fly over enemy territory. However, NF.IIs carrying the older AI.IV were, from late 1943, permitted to operate above enemy terrain when flying with ▶▶

An NF.II, DZ716/UP-L of 605 Squadron, photographed in March 1943. In April 1942 night-fighter Mosquitos had adopted an overall 'smooth' Night black finish, but in due course all night-fighter and fighter-bomber Mosquitos would adopt what became the standard 'Night Fighter Scheme' of overall Medium Sea Grey with the upper surfaces also receiving disruptive Dark Green camouflage. The Air Ministry rightly decreed that as fighter-bomber and night-fighter aircraft were built on the same production lines it was impractical to differentiate between these roles for the purpose of applying distinctive colour schemes. Peter Green

Mosquito NF.II DD739/RX-X (with radar removed) of 456 (RAAF) Squadron pictured in 1943. Crown Copyright

100 (Bomber Support) Group.

The first unit to convert to the NF.XII was 85 Squadron in March 1943, who's commanding officer was Wg Cdr John Cunningham. He would become a well-known personality as a night-fighter pilot (although he supposedly disliked his 'Cat's Eyes' nickname) and after the war as a famous test pilot with de Havilland. It is often forgotten, though, that his squadron was responsible for the operational début of centimetric radar. Aircrew from 85 scored the first NF.XII victories during the night of April 14-15, 1943, and over the next few months (along with 151, 157 and 256 Squadrons) became occupied dealing with Fw 190 fighter-bombers attacking the south of England. In July the first Messerschmitt Me 410 downed over the UK was claimed by 85, followed by the initial Junkers Ju 188 that October. The Mosquito NF.XVII entered service

Early production night-fighter NF.IIs congregate on February 12, 1942, prior to their delivery to the RAF. The examples in a line facing away from the camera are (left to right) W4090, W4092 and W4088, while the fourth aircraft further away may well be W4086. De Havilland

next, with 85 and 125 Squadrons, later in 1943.

Mid-1942 brought a new element to the fighter Mosquito story when 23 Squadron re-equipped with what was termed the NF.II (Special); two more squadrons, 605 and 418, followed suit in the early months of 1943. Here the NF.II's radar had been removed and the aircraft were used to attack troops and vehicles, airfields and other ground targets using their guns, and the first of these intruder operations took place in July 1942.

In due course 23 (then in Malta), 418 and 605 became the first squadrons to receive the FB.VI, and these were followed by 464 and 487 Squadrons operating within the newly formed 2TAF; when joined by 21 Squadron, 464 and 487 formed what was called the Sculthorpe Wing. Operations began on October 3, 1943, and the new mark would play an increasing role hitting vital tactical targets across Europe, to the extent that by the start of 1944, three more squadrons, 107, 305 and 613, had formed a second Mosquito FB.VI wing.

It was six of these Mosquitos which, on February 18, 1944, opened the walls of Amiens jail to enable imprisoned members of the French Resistance to escape. This was a classic example of the pin-point precision attacks then possible by Mosquito FB.VIs flying at very low level, though sadly during this operation the pilot leading the raid, Gp Capt Pickard (at the time well known for appearing in the famous propaganda film *Target for Tonight*) was killed along with his navigator Flt Lt Broadley. In April 1944, 613 Squadron FB.VIs hit Gestapo offices in the Hague to try and destroy records of Dutch Resistance groups. And all six FB.VI squadrons within 2TAF had major intruder roles to play in the hours and first days following the D-Day landings of June 1944.

Bomber Support

As the war progressed, ever more sophisticated airborne electrical ⟫

Improvisation: a superb photo of an NF.II undergoing maintenance under cover, away from the well-facilitated airfield hangers available in the UK. Tony Buttler Collection

equipment was developed (which sometime later would be called avionics) and, as part of this, 100 (Bomber Support) Group was formed as a radio countermeasures force. Once again the Mosquito proved to be the ideal platform and special fighter versions were produced to escort heavy bomber formations at night. During the final months of 1943, 141, 239 and then 169 Squadron – all within 100 Group – received special Mosquito Mk.IIs fitted with long-range tanks, Gee navigation and AI.IV radar working in combination with Serrate, a new device designed to home in on the transmissions produced by enemy fighters. By summer 1944 the Mk.IIs allocated to these units were being replaced by FB.VIs with similar equipment, while further FB.VIs went to 515 Squadron who's aircraft also carried an additional jamming 'black box' codenamed Moonshine.

Plans to turn 85 and 157 into bomber support squadrons were, however, disrupted when both units had to be re-assigned to undertake patrol and intercept operations against V-1 flying bombs being launched from occupied territory against the south of England – a role in which they were accompanied by 96, 219, 409 and 418 Squadrons. Here, the AI.X radar was capable of tracking these tiny targets and the Mosquitos tried to pick off the V-1s early in their flights when still close to

the French coast. Mosquitos would claim 623 V-1s destroyed in total.

Another piece of equipment, called Perfectos and designed to home onto German aircraft Identification Friend or Foe (IFF) transmissions, was employed by FB.VIs of 169 Squadron, a further Perfectos II plus the Monica VI rearward-looking radar went into 85 Squadron machines, and 23, 141 and 515 Squadrons' FB.VIs all eventually carried the American 3cm AI.XV 'ASH' radar, which replaced the nose-mounted machine guns. The NF.30 arrived next (in June 1944) to equip 219 Squadron for home defence

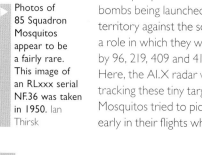

duties, but by late 1944 it became possible to release some squadrons for offensive missions. The NF.36 was extent by May 1945 but the NF.38, the last night fighter version, did not appear until after the war. Altogether 100 Group Mosquitos claimed the destruction of 267 enemy aircraft.

Overseas

The night-fighter and fighter-bomber also left their mark overseas, though not to the extent of their employment in Europe. In December 1942, 23 Squadron took its fighter NF.II (Special) airframes to Malta for operations over Sicily, and was joined in July 1943 by 256 Squadron with its Mosquito NF.XII night-fighters, all in readiness to support the Allied invasion of Sicily. During the last year of the war, 600 and 255 Squadrons, flying NF.XIXs, joined them in Italy, and towards the end of the conflict 256's NF.XIIs and XIIIs flew anti-fighter bomber-support missions.

Initially it was considered that the Mosquito's wooden structure might be vulnerable to the tropical conditions experienced in the Far East, with its wet, humid atmosphere and insects with an appetite for wood. Consequently, in mid-1943 a 'sample' NF.II airframe and an FB.VI were despatched to India for assessment, and this indicated there would not be any serious problems operating the aircraft in the Far East (although some structural issues did arise, thought largely attributable to adhesive and manufacturing flaws, which were later overcome).

The first squadron to convert was 45 with FB.VIs in February 1944 and next came 82 in July, and then 47 and 84 Squadrons arrived in early 1945. Once more the Mosquito FB.VIs were used to attack tactical targets. The peak of their effort came in May 1945 with the assault on Rangoon, while other Mosquito squadrons to move to this theatre (with either FB or

A post-war view of NF.36 RL239 of 141 Squadron. Ian Thirsk

A splendid group photo of 4 Squadron air and groundcrew and their Mosquitos. Key Collection

Line-up of 540 Squadron Mosquitos. Tony Buttler Collection

Spartan Air Services Mosquito B.35 carried the Canadian civil registration CF-HMT on its fin. Tony Buttler Collection

Groundcrew admire 'Popeye' artwork on the access hatch of a Burma-based Mosquito in 1945. Tony Buttler Collection

high-fighting performance, and it was the only type that combined great versatility of application with a performance comparable to that of the best specialised types. And it even went into civil airline service.

From 1943 until the end of the war, Mosquito FB.VIs and a single PR.IV were used by the British Overseas Airways Corporation (BOAC) as transports between Stockholm in (neutral) Sweden and the Coastal Command base at Leuchars in Scotland. Using Mosquitos allowed these 'ball-bearing' flights to be undertaken with reasonable safety, even with the very long hours of daylight available during the summer in northern Europe. The small but high-value cargoes carried by these aircraft, besides precision ball bearings and other metals, included Diplomatic Bags and VIP passengers, the latter accommodated in an improvised cabin within the bomb bay. To avoid violating Swedish neutrality, the aircrew were made 'civilian' employees of BOAC and the Mosquitos carried civil markings and registrations.

After the war the Mosquito found other civil work, especially in Canada. In 1955 Spartan Air Services based at Ottawa acquired 12 B.35s modified for high-altitude aerial survey work with a new radio, direction finding loop and a new oxygen system. These alterations were made at Derby (Burnaston) Airport prior to their ferry flights over the Atlantic and the Mosquitos worked across America in this role until the mid-1960s.

NF versions) were 89, 110, 176 and 211 (RAAF Mosquitos were of course also operating in the Far East). Post-war, some 'Mossies' were retained in the Far East, while no fewer than eight RAF Squadrons operated night-fighter versions well into the 1950s. Most of these were based back in the UK, but 39 Squadron's home was at Khartoum in North Africa and 219 was at Kabrit in Egypt.

Civil Roles
During World War Two the Mosquito offered an unrivalled combination of long range with considerable

A BOAC courier Mosquito ready to take off on its night sortie to Sweden. Tony Buttler Collection

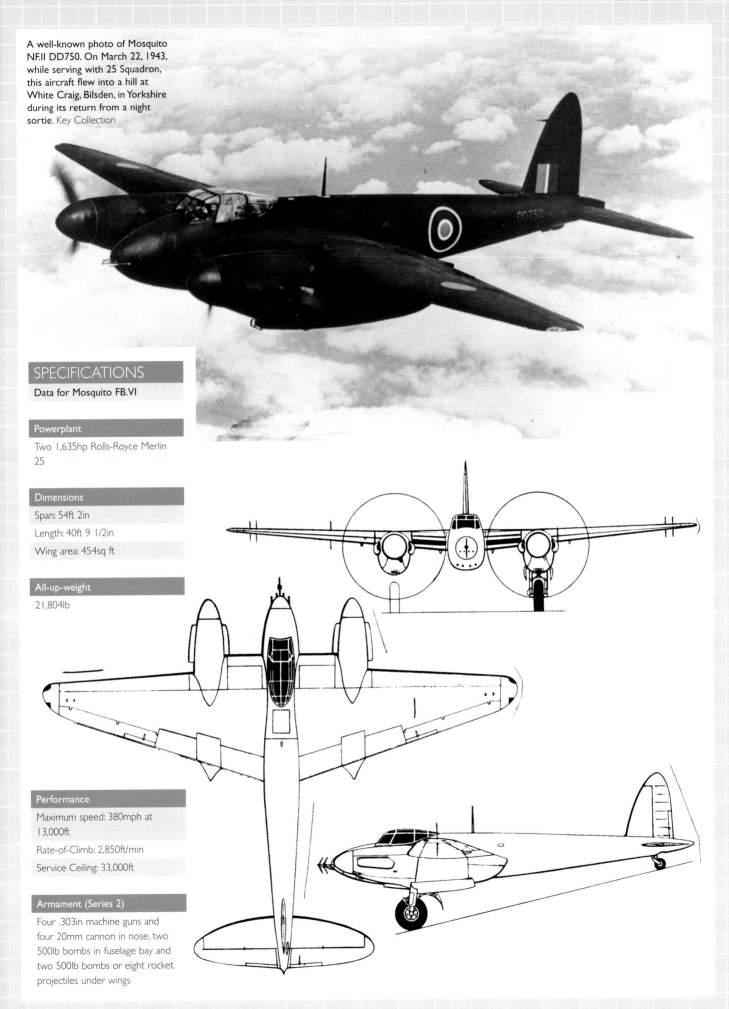

A well-known photo of Mosquito
NF.II DD750. On March 22, 1943,
while serving with 25 Squadron,
this aircraft flew into a hill at
White Craig, Bilsden, in Yorkshire
during its return from a night
sortie. Key Collection

SPECIFICATIONS

Data for Mosquito FB.VI

Powerplant

Two 1,635hp Rolls-Royce Merlin
25

Dimensions

Span: 54ft 2in

Length: 40ft 9 1/2in

Wing area: 454sq ft

All-up-weight

21,804lb

Performance

Maximum speed: 380mph at
13,000ft

Rate-of-Climb: 2,850ft/min

Service Ceiling: 33,000ft

Armament (Series 2)

Four .303in machine guns and
four 20mm cannon in nose, two
500lb bombs in fuselage bay and
two 500lb bombs or eight rocket
projectiles under wings

DE HAVILLAND MOSQUITO IV

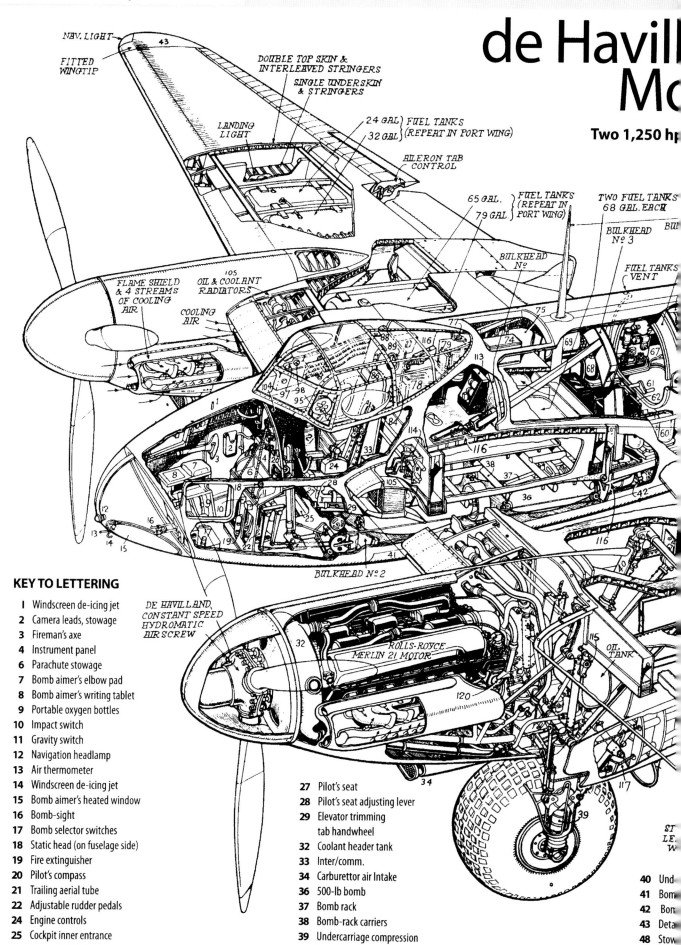

de Havill
Mo

Two 1,250 hp

NAV. LIGHT
FITTED WINGTIP

DOUBLE TOP SKIN &
INTERLEAVED STRINGERS
SINGLE UNDERSKIN
& STRINGERS

24 GAL) FUEL TANKS
32 GAL) (REPEAT IN PORT WING)

AILERON TAB
CONTROL

LANDING
LIGHT

65 GAL. FUEL TANKS
79 GAL. (REPEAT IN
PORT WING)

TWO FUEL TANKS
68 GAL. EACH

BULKHEAD
No 3

FUEL TANKS
VENT

FLAME SHIELD
& 4 STREAMS
OF COOLING
AIR

OIL & COOLANT
RADIATORS

COOLING
AIR

BULKHEAD
No

DE HAVILLAND
CONSTANT SPEED
HYDROMATIC
AIR SCREW

ROLLS-ROYCE
MERLIN 21 MOTOR

BULKHEAD No 2

OIL
TANK

KEY TO LETTERING

1 Windscreen de-icing jet
2 Camera leads, stowage
3 Fireman's axe
4 Instrument panel
6 Parachute stowage
7 Bomb aimer's elbow pad
8 Bomb aimer's writing tablet
9 Portable oxygen bottles
10 Impact switch
11 Gravity switch
12 Navigation headlamp
13 Air thermometer
14 Windscreen de-icing jet
15 Bomb aimer's heated window
16 Bomb-sight
17 Bomb selector switches
18 Static head (on fuselage side)
19 Fire extinguisher
20 Pilot's compass
21 Trailing aerial tube
22 Adjustable rudder pedals
24 Engine controls
25 Cockpit inner entrance
    door and drift sight

27 Pilot's seat
28 Pilot's seat adjusting lever
29 Elevator trimming
    tab handwheel
32 Coolant header tank
33 Inter/comm.
34 Carburettor air Intake
36 500-lb bomb
37 Bomb rack
38 Bomb-rack carriers
39 Undercarriage compression
    leg with rubber shock-pads

40 Und
41 Bom
42 Bom
43 Deta
48 Stow
49 Rear

ST
LE
W

nd
quito IV
s-Royce Merlin 21 engines

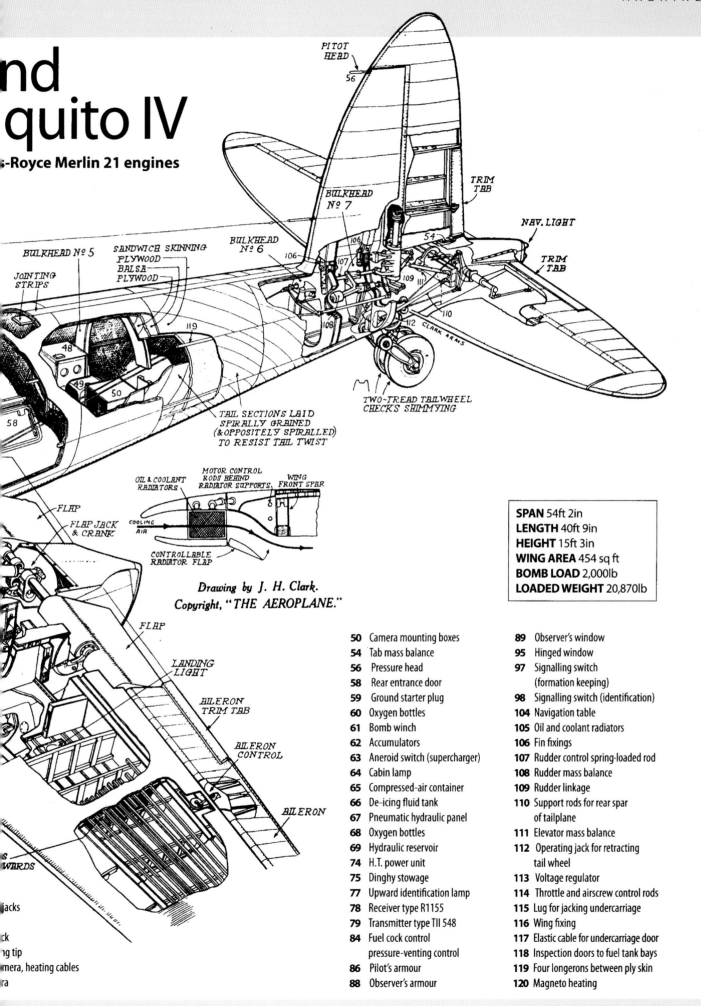

PITOT HEAD
56

BULKHEAD Nº 7

TRIM TAB

NAV. LIGHT

TRIM TAB

BULKHEAD Nº 5

SANDWICH SKINNING
PLYWOOD
BALSA
PLYWOOD

BULKHEAD Nº 6

JOINTING STRIPS

106

107

54

109 111

119

48

108

112 CLARK ARMS

110

49

50

58

TAIL SECTIONS LAID SPIRALLY GRAINED (& OPPOSITELY SPIRALLED) TO RESIST TAIL TWIST

TWO-TREAD TAILWHEEL CHECKS SHIMMYING

MOTOR CONTROL RODS BEHIND RADIATOR SUPPORTS

OIL & COOLANT RADIATORS

WING FRONT SPAR

FLAP

FLAP JACK & CRANK

COOLING AIR

CONTROLLABLE RADIATOR FLAP

Drawing by J. H. Clark.
Copyright, "THE AEROPLANE."

FLAP

LANDING LIGHT

AILERON TRIM TAB

AILERON CONTROL

s
WARDS

AILERON

jacks

k

g tip

mera, heating cables

ra

SPAN 54ft 2in			
LENGTH 40ft 9in			
HEIGHT 15ft 3in			
WING AREA 454 sq ft			
BOMB LOAD 2,000lb			
LOADED WEIGHT 20,870lb			

No	Description	No	Description
50	Camera mounting boxes	89	Observer's window
54	Tab mass balance	95	Hinged window
56	Pressure head	97	Signalling switch (formation keeping)
58	Rear entrance door		
59	Ground starter plug	98	Signalling switch (identification)
60	Oxygen bottles	104	Navigation table
61	Bomb winch	105	Oil and coolant radiators
62	Accumulators	106	Fin fixings
63	Aneroid switch (supercharger)	107	Rudder control spring-loaded rod
64	Cabin lamp	108	Rudder mass balance
65	Compressed-air container	109	Rudder linkage
66	De-icing fluid tank	110	Support rods for rear spar of tailplane
67	Pneumatic hydraulic panel		
68	Oxygen bottles	111	Elevator mass balance
69	Hydraulic reservoir	112	Operating jack for retracting tail wheel
74	H.T. power unit		
75	Dinghy stowage	113	Voltage regulator
77	Upward identification lamp	114	Throttle and airscrew control rods
78	Receiver type R1155	115	Lug for jacking undercarriage
79	Transmitter type TII 548	116	Wing fixing
84	Fuel cock control pressure-venting control	117	Elastic cable for undercarriage door
		118	Inspection doors to fuel tank bays
86	Pilot's armour	119	Four longerons between ply skin
88	Observer's armour	120	Magneto heating

RECCE STAR

Among the important roles performed by the Mosquito in World War Two was photo-reconnaissance. **Malcolm V Lowe** tells the story of the recce Mosquitos and their significant contribution to victory

The first recce Mosquito, and therefore the first Mosquito taken on charge by the RAF, was the second prototype, W4051. It flew with 1 PRU coded 'LY-U', and had the fuselage of a production PR.I airframe.
Malcolm V Lowe Collection

twin-engined Lockheed 12A (civil registered G-AFTL), he was able to clandestinely overfly military installations, notably in Nazi Germany.

Cotton set to work championing the need for a fast, twin-engined camera-carrying platform, and gained sufficient official interest to begin the creation of suitable recce airframes using existing and new types.

Covert adaptations

Much of Cotton's subsequent conversion work and prototype flying at RAF Heston airfield was carried out under strict security. Cotton was made an acting wing commander, and his activities later went under the cover name of 2 Camouflage Unit. Eventually this pioneering work was formally renamed as the Photographic Development Unit (PDU) at Heston - and later RAF Benson, Oxfordshire, became a major hub of RAF recce activities. The PDU subsequently gave birth, during July 1940, to the Photographic Reconnaissance Unit (PRU), the first of several such specialist organisations within the RAF at home and in other war zones. Relocated to Benson late in 1940, the PRU was renamed 1 PRU, and it became significant in the recce Mosquito story.

The initial Mosquito prototype, W4050, made its maiden flight on November 25, 1940. But of great importance for the recce development of the Mosquito was the second prototype, W4051. This aircraft was built, like the prototype, at Salisbury Hall, Hertfordshire. It first flew on June 10, 1941. An early camera layout for this aircraft was recorded as being three ubiquitous ▶▶

The PR.XVI was among the main wartime production models of the Mosquito that utilised two-stage Merlin engines. This beautiful in-flight image shows NS502/M of 544 Squadron, RAF during July 1944, wearing full 'Invasion Stripes'.
Malcolm V Lowe Collection

Distinctive red and white diagonal tail stripes, plus yellow spinners, identified the recce Mosquitos of San Severo-based 60 Squadron, SAAF. The black and white fuselage stripes were a recognition feature during the invasion of southern France for these Mediterranean-based camera-carriers. SAAF

One of the key ingredients of the eventual Allied victory in Europe during May 1945 was photo-reconnaissance. Intelligence-gathering regarding many aspects of the enemy's war machine and locations of significant targets had grown into a major part of Allied wartime activities. This included a large contribution from the RAF's recce assets. Key among these was the Mosquito, which was developed during the war years into a pre-eminent camera-carrying platform, especially in fast high-level photography.

Immediate need

The massive effort of RAF photo-recce by the latter stages of World War Two was in stark contrast to the situation that existed when the conflict began in September 1939. At that time the RAF did not possess a dedicated or specialised recce or photo-intelligence organisation. Recce was expected to be carried out by such types as Bristol Blenheims and even Westland Lysanders. Clearly these types were no match for Luftwaffe fighters or other defences,

especially if flown alone without strong fighter cover. They also did not possess the range necessary to fly deep into enemy territory, and were therefore at best simply tactical intelligence-gathering platforms.

However, ground-breaking work by several individuals was to transform this situation from the later 1930s onwards. Chief among them was a civilian named Sidney Cotton.

An Australian by birth, Cotton specialised in several fields, notably aerial photography. Pre-war, using a specially converted camera-carrying

The US Eighth Air Force was allocated at least 145 Mosquito PR.XVIs, many being flown by the 25th Bomb Group (R) at RAF Watton. The red 'tail feathers' were to avoid possible friendly fire. This PR.XVI, MM345/Z, belonged to the 653rd Bomb Squadron. Malcolm V Lowe Collection

F.24 aerial cameras mounted vertically in the fuselage together with one oblique camera.

Such was the importance attached to the development of the Mosquito as a long-range camera platform that an initial order for bomber Mosquitos was modified to include nine specialist recce airframes designated Mosquito PR.Mk.I. Although there had initially been much scepticism in official circles as to the merit of the 'Mossie', wartime necessity proved the overriding need for the aircraft, and the success of specially converted Spitfires on long-range as

well as shorter-haul recce flights had shown the undoubted value of the intelligence so obtained.

Similar to W4051, the PR.Is were austere airframes compared to later production Mosquitos, among distinguishing points they had engine nacelles shorter than most production Mosquitos. Along with the prototype W4051, they all served with the RAF, four having additional fuel tankage for long-range recce sorties.

On July 13, 1941, W4051 was delivered to 1 PRU at Benson, which by then had become the centre of RAF recce activities. It

therefore became the first Mosquito of any mark to join the RAF, and subsequently flew the first successful Mosquito recce sortie on September 17, 1941, when it was used for a flight from Benson all the way to the Franco-Spanish border and back. Subsequent sorties were flown to many places of interest, with W4051 being joined by several further PR.Is in the following months. Places visited by these early machines included the major German naval base at Kiel, and the French coast prior to the Commando raid on Saint-Nazaire (Operation Chariot) in March 1942.

Powered by two single-stage Merlin XXI engines, the PR.I had a maximum speed of some 382mph, a ceiling of 35,000ft, and a range of approximately 2,510 miles.

This pioneering batch of early production Mosquitos was a great success, and laid the foundations for the Mosquito to become one of the most important recce aircraft of all time. Indeed, from the earliest days, the excellent performance of the unarmed camera-carrying Mosquitos allowed most to evade trouble and outrun enemy fighters.

Such was the success of the initial recce Mosquitos that some 30

Forward fuselage and engine nacelle detail of Mosquito PR.XVI MM356. The two-stage Merlins of this mark were distinguishable by the extra 'chin' intake just below the spinner. A camera 'window' is just visible at the forward end of the bomb bay housing. BAE Systems

A silver-painted Mosquito PR.34, RG314, shows off the classic lines of this late-manufacture mark of recce Mosquito. The PR.34/34a served with the RAF well into the jet era post-World War Two, only retiring in the mid-1950s. Key Collection

Mosquito B.IV Series II bombers were converted into PR.IV camera-carrying examples. The first operational flight by a PR.IV is generally regarded to have been made by DK284 during April 1942.

Power upgrade

Up to this point in recce Mosquito conversion/production, all marks had been powered by 'single-stage' Merlins. This meant the engine had a straightforward single-stage supercharger. Such an arrangement had served the Mosquito well thus far, but continuing development work at Rolls-Royce had led to a more powerful Merlin. This was fitted with a two-stage supercharger, and was the basis of a large family of Merlin powerplants of various capacities and capabilities. In particular, the development of the two-speed, two-stage supercharged Merlin was a significant step forward in aero engine performance and became important for the Mosquito.

This was firstly manifested in 60-series Merlin engines, but from the 70-series onwards they were a standard fit. These new-generation Merlins gave enhanced performance envelopes for both the Spitfire and Mosquito, which could fly higher and faster, thus making them increasingly difficult to intercept and allowing them

to complete their vital intelligence-gathering activities relatively unhindered at greater ranges.

Initial developments

The Merlin 61 was the first production version of the Merlin to be fitted with a two-stage supercharger. For development work leading to the two-stage Merlin's introduction into Mosquito production, the original prototype, W4050, played an important part. It first flew with two Merlin 61s fitted during June 1942. The performance figures achieved by this aircraft with the new engines were impressive by mid-1942 standards, with a top speed of some

437mph above 29,000ft.

The first RAF Mosquitos with the new breed of two-speed, two-stage Merlins were, appropriately, recce-configured examples. The Mosquito PR.VIII, built as a stop-gap pending the introduction of the intended main production PR.IX, was the first recce model fitted with two-stage Merlins. The five PR.VIIIs were converted from B.IV bombers and were fitted with Merlin 61 engines of 1,565hp at 11,250ft (according to contemporary official figures) in place of the single-stage Merlins of the B.IV bomber variant. The first PR.VIII flew during October 1942. The type could reach in the region of a very creditable ⟫

Dark blue spinners distinguished Mosquitos of the 653rd Bomb Squadron, 25th Bomb Group (R) of the Eighth Air Force, based at RAF Watton. The 'Mighty Eighth' was a major user of the PR.XVI, exemplified here by NS739/F. Malcolm V Lowe Collection

Recce Mosquitos served world-wide with the RAF, both during and after World War Two. This post-war PR.XVI, NS645 of 684 Squadron, was photographed at Alipore, India. JB via Malcolm V Lowe

350mph at around 30,000ft, and had an excellent service ceiling of some 38,000ft.

Enhanced variants

The first production Mosquitos built from the start with the two-stage Merlin as standard were the B.IX bomber and PR.IX recce aircraft, these two marks being basically similar apart from their obviously different mission equipment and fittings.

Altogether, 90 examples of the Mosquito PR.IX are known to have been manufactured. The first of these, LR405, initially flew during April 1943. The PR.IX was powered similarly to the B.IX, with Merlin 76/77 engines, their performance figures (according to Rolls-Royce data) being of 1,655hp at 10,000ft, there being specific Merlin sub-types for port and starboard wing installation where required. The 70-series Merlin was the main new

two-speed Merlin production engine, moving on from the initial 60-series units.

A major distinguishing feature of two-stage Merlin-equipped Mosquitos was the new, prominent 'chin' air intake below the propeller spinner at the extreme front of the lower engine cowling.

Increased capability

Continuing development led to even more powerful and potent Mosquito variants; the B.XVI bomber and closely-related PR.XVI recce platform were both highly important to the RAF in the war's later stages. The PR.XVI was a major step forward towards the ultimate Mosquito recce configuration. It had a pressurised cockpit for its two crew members and, similar to the PR.IX, was powered by two Rolls-Royce Merlin 76/77 engines. The initial example

flew during July 1943. This variant was equipped with overload fuel tanks in the bomb bay to extend its range, and could also carry different sizes of underwing drop tanks. Illustrating their significance and usefulness, a total of 435 PR.XVIs were built. The type had a maximum speed of some 415mph, and a range of more than 2,800 miles.

The success of the initial PR operations with both Spitfires and Mosquitos led to a significant expansion of the RAF's recce assets and activities. Aircraft assigned to 1 PRU were based not only at Benson, but at Wick and Leuchars in Scotland, St Eval in Cornwall and overseas at Gibraltar. The original 1 PRU was eventually split into five operational squadrons from October 1942 onwards, these being 540, 541, 542, 543 and 544 Squadrons. Their Mosquitos ranged far and wide over Occupied Europe and provided a wealth of imagery for the photographic interpreters at RAF Medmenham.

The Mosquito increasingly took over the long-range photographic role from the Spitfire, which was more suited to shorter-range operations. Eventually Mosquito sorties were flown not just by day but at night as well, using special photoflash 'bombs', which provided sufficient illumination for excellent images to be made even on the darkest nights.

Although a large number of sorties

The second Mosquito built, W4051, while undergoing trials. It later served with 1 PRU, 521 and 540 Squadrons. Malcolm V Lowe Collection

were flown in support of Bomber Command's nocturnal bombing campaign, not all PR Mosquitos were used to photograph potential targets, or to give post-strike assessments. Many flights were made to provide vital intelligence information of the enemy's dispositions and movements as a part of the overall Allied intelligence effort. This information-gathering process grew during the war into a significant instrument of the Allies' overall success.

The final mark of recce Mosquito to make a significant combat presence during World War Two was the PR.32. This was an extended-span, long-range, high-altitude pressurised derivative of the PR.XVI. It was powered by a pair of two-stage supercharged Merlin 113/114 engines of 1,690hp at 13,000ft (Rolls-Royce figures). The initial PR.32 flew in August 1944; all five examples completed were conversions from PR.XVIs. Although small in number, these special Mosquitos were very active in the final months of the war, alongside PR.IXs and PR.XVIs photographing many potential strategic as well as tactical targets in Germany, as the Allies advanced towards final victory in Europe.

American employment

Additional to the RAF, a major user of late mark Mosquitos was the US Army Air Force(s). Specifically the Eighth Air Force in England flew various examples of the PR.XVI from the first half of 1944 onwards. Historian Roger Freeman identified at least 145 Mosquitos that were employed by the 'Mighty Eighth' at one time or another until the end of the war.

The 653rd Bomb Squadron (BS) of the 25th Bomb Group (Reconnaissance) based at RAF Watton, Norfolk, used the type primarily for weather recce and chaff dispensing. However, that group's 654th BS flew night photographic sorties among other specialist tasks. The squadron used a small number of specially converted H2X-equipped PR.XVI examples for radar scope photographic flights. A camera installation within the cockpit was rigged up to allow images to be made of the H2X scope on the flight deck.

Several USAAF Mosquitos were employed on secretive special operations work, fitted with relevant apparatus for picking up radio transmissions from ground-based agents in Occupied Europe and sometimes carrying a third crew member for this task. Both the British Special Operations Executive (SOE) and the American Office of Strategic Services (OSS) had been training agents for this purpose. Codenamed 'Red Stocking', these operations particularly suited the Mosquito. In theory, such sorties had to be flown at around 30,000ft to allow signals from ground-based agents to be intercepted successfully using a system code named Joan-Eleanor. A specialist unit, the 492nd Bomb Group at RAF Harrington, Northamptonshire, eventually flew such dangerous but vital operations.

These special duties Mosquitos were converted for carrying a third »

An in-flight view of the first recce Mosquito, W4051, the second 'Mossie' ever built. It is wearing the codes 'LY-U' of 1 PRU, but later it was assigned to 521 and 540 Squadrons. Key Collection

Among the tasks assigned to USAAF Mosquitos was clandestine work operating in conjunction with special operations personnel, for example picking up radio messages from agents in Occupied Europe. This mainly black-painted PR.XVI coded 'K' was photographed near the conflict's end. Malcolm V Lowe Collection

An example of the original batch of Mosquito PR.I airframes was W4059/LY-T, which flew with 1 PRU. Delivered to that unit during September 1941, it later operated with 540 Squadron and was struck off charge in September 1944. JB via Malcolm V Lowe

crew member, the radio operator's access being through a small door cut into the starboard side of the rear fuselage. He was provided with a very necessary heated suit and had an interphone link with the pilot. The Mosquitos' wing-mounted fuel tanks gave sufficient range for most of these sorties, but for very long-range operations – or if particularly long endurance was needed – the Mosquitos could continue on to a suitable airfield in Italy.

Springbok recce

In the Mediterranean theatre, a specialist photographic unit was 60 Squadron, South African Air Force. Already used to recce sorties using converted Martin Marylands and Baltimores, the unit received its first two Mosquitos in January 1943 while based in Libya. These were 'second-hand' Mosquito NF.II night-fighters, which the unit had to convert into recce platforms with the help of local Maintenance Unit specialists. The first sorties with these modified aircraft were made during February 1943 from the squadron's base at Castel Benito. Eventually more suitable Mosquitos reached the unit, the first PR.IX, LR411, arriving at the new base of Ariana in Tunisia during July. Although by then the fighting in North Africa had ceased, that area was still the main base for Allied aerial assets while attention turned towards invading the Italian mainland. The squadron subsequently used its new Mosquitos to make raid assessment photograph sorties over the Romanian oilfields and refineries, which had been attacked by USAAF heavy bombers.

The first photo sortie over Germany

itself was made on November 1, 1943. During the following month the squadron moved at last from North Africa to the Italian mainland, arriving at the Foggia complex of airfields in the part of Italy by then liberated and working with the Allies. From January 1944 the unit was based at San Severo, its home until just after the end of the war. A large part of southern Europe, northern Italy, the Balkans, plus Central Europe were the areas of specific activity for the squadron's Mosquitos.

A major upgrade in capability came during February 1944 with the arrival of the unit's first Mosquito PR.XVI. This excellent recce platform

subsequently formed the major part of 60 Squadron's equipment, although PR.IXs also continued to be flown. On April 4 one of the unit's Mk.IXs reconnoitred several industrial locations in Poland. While doing so the crew unwittingly photographed for the first time the Auschwitz concentration camp, although tragically the meaning of the resulting images was not realised at the time by photo interpreters.

On August 15, 1944, a 60 Squadron Mosquito (PR.XVI NS520) was photographing the Luftwaffe airfield of Leipheim at 30,000ft when it was intercepted by a Messerschmitt Me 262, one of the first times that an Allied aircraft had been involved in combat with the new German jet fighter. Pilot Capt Salomon Pienaar successfully evaded several attacks by the Messerschmitt, and although the Mosquito was damaged he successfully brought it back to San Severo.

Accidental interceptions by USAAF fighters led to the squadron adopting distinctive diagonal red and white tail stripes, making their Mosquitos among the most colourful examples of their type. The unit continued on its vital role of aerial photography until the end of the war. Losses were

Mosquito PR.34 VL619 banks for the camera to show its multiple camera 'windows' in the bulged lower fuselage. It was assigned to 13 Squadron at RAF Fayid in Egypt. Key Collection

Continuing development of the two-stage Merlin-powered recce Mosquito led on from the highly successful PR.XVI to the PR.34, as exemplified here by VL619. This mark had a bulged lower fuselage for more fuel and revised camera mountings, and could carry 200gal underwing drop tanks. The type served the RAF chiefly post-war. *Key Collection*

comparatively high, including accidents attributed to engine failure, and the growing menace of high-altitude interception by Me 262s.

The unit returned to South Africa in August 1945, taking a number of Mosquitos with it, although most of these were later stored and withdrawn from use.

Continuing operations

After the war ended, two-stage Merlin-powered Mosquitos persisted in service even into the jet era, the RAF continuing to use a variety of Mosquito variants including newer recce models developed late in World War Two.

The Mosquito PR.34 and related PR.34a were extreme-range, high-altitude photo-reconnaissance versions. The cockpit and fuel tank armour of previous marks were largely removed. Additional fuel was carried in a bulged lower fuselage and two large 200gal fuel tanks under the outer wings gave a potential (and impressive) range of 3,600 miles at a cruising speed of 300mph. The type was powered by two 1,690hp Merlins as first used in the PR.32. Most sources agree that 181 were built, including construction by Percival Aircraft at Luton (although some were started as PR.XVIs and altered on the production line). The PR.34's

maximum speed was recorded at an equally commendable 425mph at 30,000ft, and its camera fit could include four split F.52 vertical cameras in the bulged lower fuselage, and one F.24 oblique camera. A K-17 camera could be carried for aerial survey work. Dating from the summer and autumn of 1945, the PR.34a was the final Mosquito recce model, powered by the Merlin 113A/114A.

Post-war RAF operations included much recce work in the Middle and Far East. The troubles in Palestine were reconnoitred by locally

based Mosquitos including those of 680 Squadron (which was later renumbered 13 Squadron). The long-standing conflict over Malaya also brought the RAF's Mosquitos into action. There the eventually successful action against communist inspired and backed terrorists during Operation 'Firedog' resulted in the Mosquitos providing much intelligence. It was in that area that the final RAF operational Mosquito flight was made, by Singapore-based PR.34a RG314 of 81 Squadron on December 15, 1955.

The USAAF employed Mosquitos for various tasks. This PR.XVI, MM388/H, was flown by the 654th Bomb Squadron of the 25th Bomb Group (R) based at RAF Watton, in the closing months of the war. *Malcolm V Lowe Collection*

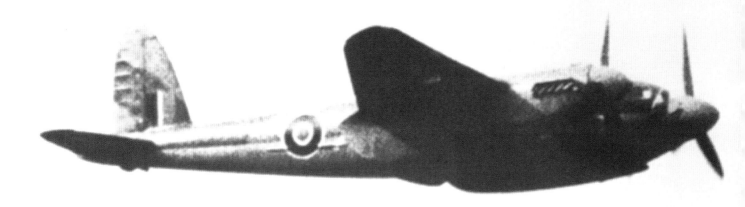

Related to 'Upkeep', the famous so-called bouncing bomb of Dambusters fame, 'Highball' was intended to be effective against specific military targets. **Malcolm V Lowe** describes the Mosquito's association with this secret weapon

A Mosquito B.IV shortly after letting go its Highball during testing. The weapon was given backspin prior to release, and had to be dropped at no more than around **60ft** above the water's surface. (Malcolm V Lowe Collection)

IN A SPIN

T he problem of successfully attacking precise, small but high-value military installations taxed the minds of armed forces and scientific personnel during World War Two. Unlike nowadays, guided weapons were in their infancy during the 1940s, and so other means had to be found for delivering useful ordnance onto a required target with the maximum effect.

The famous bouncing bomb, made legendary by 617 Squadron and its Lancasters to breach the Ruhr dams in May 1943, successfully demonstrated the melding of clever science with exceptional airmanship. Codenamed 'Upkeep', the large weapon of Dambusters lore was however not the only spinning, water-bouncing weapon that equipped RAF aircraft during the war. Also developed by Barnes Wallis and his talented team of scientists and practical creators was a related bomb named 'Highball'.

A key development airframe in the Highball programme was Mosquito B.IV DK290/G. The aircraft carried two inert Highballs in its converted bomb bay/ lower fuselage and was much photographed and filmed during its trials work. Tony Buttler Collection

This weapon was deliberately of smaller size dimensionally than Upkeep, so it could be fitted in a small but powerful airframe best suited to pin-point precision attacks on specific targets at low level. The aircraft of choice to deliver it was the Mosquito, its performance and fuselage size being capable of taking up to two of these specialised stores. But despite its more diminutive stature, Highball was potentially no less deadly than Upkeep. However, developing it and making it work effectively proved highly problematic.

Difficult trials

Initial testing of Highball prototype versions was carried out in early 1943, at Dorset's Chesil Beach and at Reculver in Kent. These trials included the modified Mosquito B.IV development aircraft DK290/G ('G' meaning the aircraft had to be guarded while on the ground because of its secret equipment). Further tests were then flown by specially-configured Mosquitos based at RAF Turnberry in Scotland against a moored target ship (the former French battleship *Courbet*) in Loch Striven.

However, modifications were needed – especially to the release mechanism – which proved time-consuming. Like Upkeep, Highball had to be spun prior to release from the Mosquito carrier aircraft, and perfecting this process was challenging. In the first half of 1944, tests were carried out on a revised version of Highball, again at Loch Striven but this time against the reserve battleship HMS *Malaya*. At least one Highball successfully (but unintentionally) made a hole in the ship's side. During May 1944, two inert

Highball prototypes were dropped as a pair for the first time from the same aircraft with just a one second delay. This was deemed the most effective delivery combination.

In its later, virtually operational form, Highball was a spherical shape with flattened sides. Its explosive filling was Torpex, enclosed in a cylinder within the casing, which was similar to the layout designed for Upkeep. The weapon was detonated by a single hydrostatic pistol, set to fire at a depth in the water of some 27ft. ⏩

Unusual deck cargo. The Mosquitos and personnel of 618 Squadron were transported to Australia in late 1944 for the possible use of Highball against Japanese targets. The two Royal Navy aircraft carriers involved, HMS *Fencer* (left) and HMS *Striker* are seen here with some of the Mosquitos on their decks.
Royal Australian Navy

Underside view of Mosquito B.IV test aircraft DK290/G. The arrangement of the two Highballs can be clearly seen, set into the specially-converted bomb bay with its prominent fairing.
Crown Copyright

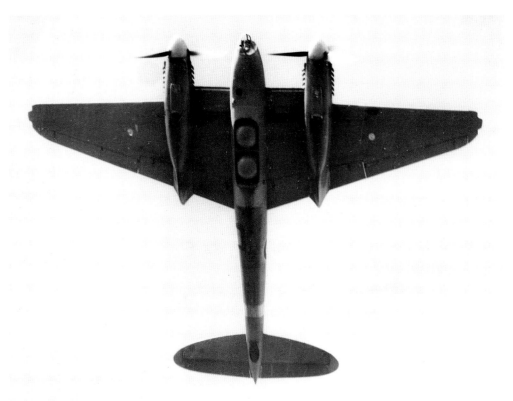

use against Japanese maritime targets. The unit's specially-converted Highball Mosquitos were transported aboard the aircraft carriers HMS *Fencer* and *Striker* via Gibraltar and Ceylon, with de Havilland Australia personnel duly making them ready for flight. Training subsequently took place at the Royal Australian Air Force (RAAF) Station Narromine, New South Wales, the unit being active there from February 1945 onwards. But in the event 618 Squadron was never used against Japanese shipping, and was disbanded at Narromine during July 1945. The specially-converted Mosquitos were stripped of their military equipment and eventually sold… a sad end to a promising but eventually totally unfulfilled operational capability.

American connection

In January 1945, a USAAF Douglas A-26 Invader was adapted by Vickers technicians to carry two Highballs. They were almost completely enclosed in the bomb bay, using parts from a Mosquito conversion. After brief flight testing in the UK, the kit was sent across the Atlantic to Wright Field, Ohio, and installed in an A-26C Invader. Twenty-five inert Highballs, apparently known to the Americans as 'Speedee' bombs, were dispatched to the US for use in the USAAF trials. Release tests were carried out over Choctawhatchee Bay near Eglin Field, Florida. Tragically, on April 28, 1945 during a drop test, the inert Speedee bounced dangerously and struck the Invader, breaking its fuselage apart and causing it to crash fatally. The project was subsequently abandoned. ◗

Its weight was in the region of 1,280lb, of which some 600lb was Torpex. Carried inside a special fairing within the aircraft's converted bomb bay/lower fuselage, before release Highball was spun backwards at 700-900rpm with power supplied by a ram air turbine mounted in the bomb bay's mid-section, served by an extendable air intake. The bombs were intended to be dropped from a maximum altitude of approximately 60ft and at a speed of around 360mph.

Frontline intentions

To use Highball operationally, 618 Squadron RAF had been formed on April 1, 1943 at RAF Skitten, near Wick in Scotland. The unit was primarily tasked to undertake Operation Servant, in which the German battleship *Tirpitz* would be attacked with Highball bouncing bombs at its Norwegian hiding place. However, delays with the development and delivery means of Highball prevented the squadron from employing the weapon operationally. The unit was equipped with various marks of bomber Mosquito, most importantly including B.IVs, which had been specially converted to carry Highball, with the associated necessarily complicated release gear. The unit also flew the Mosquito B.VI and B.XVI among other types.

If Highball had been made ready in time, it would have been used against the German capital ship Tirpitz *at its Norwegian hideaway. The trials Mosquito B.IV DK290/G (G = 'Guard') shown here carried two inert Highballs for the camera.* Crown Copyright

In the event, Highball was never used by 618 Squadron or indeed by any other unit. Although seemingly a good idea, the main reason for its existence was removed in spectacular fashion. On November 12, 1944 Operation Catechism was carried out. Lancasters of 9 and 617 Squadrons with 'Tallboy' (Bomb, Medium Capacity, 12,000lb) earthquake bombs sank Highball's primary target, the German battleship *Tirpitz*. Although other potential targets had been considered during Highball's development, none of these proved practicable or, eventually, necessary.

However, in late 1944, 618 Squadron was deployed to Australia for possible

The sad sight of former 618 Squadron RAF Highball Mosquitos 'put out to pasture' at RAAF Station Narromine, New South Wales, awaiting sale and with parts already missing from some aircraft. They never flew in action against German or Japanese targets. Key Collection

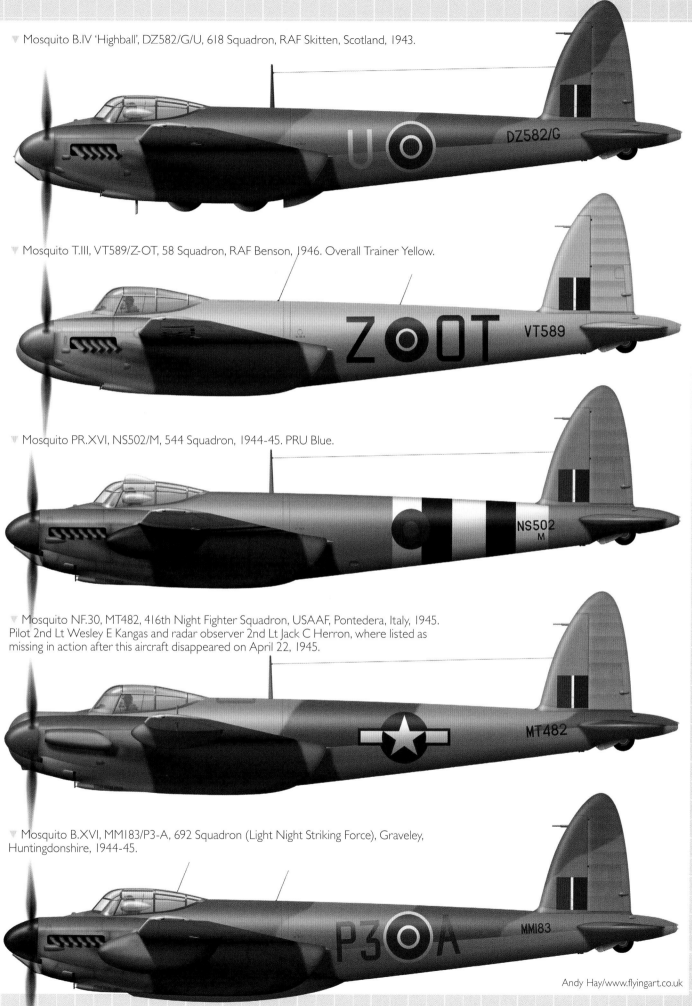

▼ Mosquito B.IV 'Highball', DZ582/G/U, 618 Squadron, RAF Skitten, Scotland, 1943.

▼ Mosquito T.III, VT589/Z-OT, 58 Squadron, RAF Benson, 1946. Overall Trainer Yellow.

▼ Mosquito PR.XVI, NS502/M, 544 Squadron, 1944-45. PRU Blue.

▼ Mosquito NF.30, MT482, 416th Night Fighter Squadron, USAAF, Pontedera, Italy, 1945.
Pilot 2nd Lt Wesley E Kangas and radar observer 2nd Lt Jack C Herron, where listed as
missing in action after this aircraft disappeared on April 22, 1945.

▼ Mosquito B.XVI, MM183/P3-A, 692 Squadron (Light Night Striking Force), Graveley,
Huntingdonshire, 1944-45.

Andy Hay/www.flyingart.co.uk

BRITISH SQUADRON/UNIT LIST
RAF AND ROYAL NAVY

This list includes those Royal Australian Air Force (RAAF), Royal Canadian Air Force (RCAF), Royal New Zealand Air Force (RNZAF), Norwegian Air Force and Polish Air Force squadrons based during the war both in the UK and in the European theatre and operating under British control.

Note: some units given here were only partially equipped with Mosquitos or had just a small number on strength (for example, 617 Squadron).

References: Air-Britain's The Squadrons of the RAF and Commonwealth (Halley), The Squadrons of the Fleet Air Arm (Sturtivant and Ballance) and RAF Flying Training and Support Units since 1912 (Sturtivant with Hamlin). Also Mosquito: The Illustrated History (Birtles) and Combat Codes (Flintham and Thomas).

Royal Air Force

4 Squadron
B.XVI 1.44 to 6.44
FB.VI 9.45 to 7.50
Code: None until 1945, UP afterwards

8 Squadron
FB.VI 9.46 to 4.47
Code: RT

11 Squadron
FB.VI 10.48 to 8.50
Code: EX

13 Squadron
PR.34 9.46 to 2.52
Code: None

14 Squadron
B.VI 6.45 to 3.46
B.XVI 4.46 to 7.48
B.35 12.47 to 3.51
Code: CX

18 Squadron
Met.VI 3.47 to 11.47
Code: WV

21 Squadron
B.IV 9.43 to 10.47
Code: YH

22 Squadron
FB.VI 5.46 to 8.46
Code: None

23 Squadron
NF.II 7.42 to 9.43
FB.VI 5.43 to 9.45
NF.30 9.46 to 2.47
NF.36 2.47 to 6.52
Code: YP

29 Squadron
NF.XII 5.43 to 4.44
NF.XIII 10.43 to 2.45
NF.30 2.45 to 8.46, 10.50 to 8.51
NF.36 8.46 to 10.50
Code: RO

36 Squadron
FB.VI 10.46 to 10.47
Code: DM

39 Squadron
FB.VI 2.46 to 9.46
NF.36 3.49 to 3.53
Code: None

Royal New Zealand Air Force Mosquito MM417/EG-T, of 487 Squadron, is pictured during a daylight bombing sortie in 1944. *Crown Copyright*

45 Squadron
FB.VI 2.44 to 5.46
Code: OB

46 Squadron
NF.XII 7.44 to 12.44
Code: None

47 Squadron
FB.VI 10.44 to 11.44, 2.45 to 3.46
Code: KU

55 Squadron
FB.26 6.46 to 11.46
Code: None

58 Squadron
PR.16 and PR.34 10.46 to 11.47, 1.49 to 12.54
PR.35 10.51 to 3.54
Code: OT

68 Squadron
NF.XVII and NF.XIX 7.44 to 2.45
NF.30 2.45 to 4.45
Code: WM

69 Squadron
PR.1 1.42 to 3.42
FB.VI 8.45 to 3.46
B.XVI 4.46 to 11.47
Code: WI

81 Squadron
PR.XVI 9.46
PR.34 9.46 to 12.55
Code: None

82 Squadron
FB.VI 7.44 to 3.46
Code: UX

84 Squadron
FB.VI 2.45 to 11.46
Code: PY

85 Squadron
NF.II 8.42 to 7.43
NF.XII 3.43 to 11.44
NF.XIII 10.43 to 5.44
NF.XV 3.43 to 8.43
NF.XVII 11.43 to 5.44
NF.30 11.44 to 4.46
NF.36 1.46 to 10.51
Code: VY

89 Squadron
FB.VI 2.45 to 4.45
NF.XIX 4.45 to 3.46
Code: None

96 Squadron
NF.XII 6.43 to 8.43
NF.XIII 8.43 to 12.44
Code: ZJ

FB.VI LR366/OM-L of 107 Squadron displays D-Day stripe markings on its lower fuselage.

98 Squadron
B.XVI 11.45 to 8.48
B.35 8.48 to 2.51
Code: VO

105 Squadron
B.IV 11.41 to 3.44
B.IX 7.43 to 2.46
B.XVI 3.44 to 2.46
Code: GB

107 Squadron
B.VI 2.44 to 9.48
Code: OM

108 Squadron
NF.XII 2.44 to 7.44
Code: None

109 Squadron
B.IV 8.42 to 6.44
B.IX 6.43 to 9.45
B.XVI 3.44 to 12.48
B.35 4.48 to 7.52
Code: HS

110 Squadron
FB.VI 11.44 to 4.46
Code: VE

114 Squadron
FB.VI 11.45 to 9.46
Code: RT

125 Squadron
NF.XVII 2.44 to 3.45
NF.30 2.45 to 11.45
Code: VA

128 Squadron
B.XVI 11.44 to 4.46
B.XX 9.44 to 11.44
B.25 10.44 to 11.44
Code: M5

139 Squadron
B.IV 9.42 to 7.44
B.IX 9.43 to 9.44
B.XVI 2.44 to 11.48
B.XX 11.43 to 9.45
B.25 9.44 to 9.45
B.35 10.48 to 12.53
Code: XD

140 Squadron
B.IX 11.43 to 12.44
PR.XVI 12.43 to 7.45
Code: None

141 Squadron
NF.II 10.43 to 8.44
FB.VI 7.44 to 3.45
NF.30 3.45 to 9.45
NF.36 6.46 to 12.51
Code: TW

142 Squadron
B.25 10.44 to 9.45
B.35 8.45 to 9.45
Code: 4H

143 Squadron
NF.II 10.44 to 1.45
FB.VI 10.44 to 5.45
Code: NE

151 Squadron
NF.II 4.42 to 8.43
FB.VI 8.43 to 10.43
NF.XII 5.43 to 5.44
NF.XIII 11.43 to 11.44
NF.30 10.44 to 10.46
Code: DZ

157 Squadron
NF.II 1.42 to 7.44
FB.VI 7.43 to 4.44
NF.XIX 5.44 to 8.45
NF.30 2.45 to 8.45
Code: RS

162 Squadron
FB.VI 10.43 to 1.44
B.XX and B.25 12.44 to 7.46
Code: CR

163 Squadron
B.XVI 5.45 to 8.45
B.25 1.45 to 5.45
Code: ZI

169 Squadron
NF.II 1.44 to 7.44
FB.VI 6.44 to 8.45
NF.XIX 1.45 to 8.45
Code: VI

176 Squadron
B.XVI 6.45 to 7.45
B.XIX 7.45 to 5.46
Code: None

180 Squadron
B.XVI 9.45 to 5.46
Code: EV

Mosquito NF.36 night-fighter RL139/TW-P of 141 Squadron. Ian Thirsk

Mosquito HK382 was an NF.XIII night-fighter and here is seen serving as RO-T of 29 Squadron at RAF Hunsdon in Hertfordshire. Tony Buttler Collection

192 Squadron
B.IV 1.43 to 8.45
B.XVI 2.45 to 8.45
Code: DT

199 Squadron
NF.36 12.51 to 3.54
Code: None

211 Squadron
FB.VI 6.45 to 3.46
Code: None

219 Squadron
NF.XVII 2.44 to 12.44
NF.30 6.44 to 9.46
NF.36 3.51 to 11.52
Code: FK

235 Squadron
FB.VI 6.44 to 7.45
Code: LA

239 Squadron
NF.II 12.43 to 1.45
FB.VI 9.44 to 1.45
NF.30 1.45 to 7.45
Code: HB

248 Squadron
FB.VI 12.43 to 9.46
FB.XVIII 1.44 to 2.45
Code: DM

249 Squadron
FB.26 3.46 to 8.46
Code: GN

254 Squadron
FB.XVIII 4.45 to 5.45
Code: QM

255 Squadron
NF.XIX 1.45 to 4.46
NF.30 4.45 to 4.46
Code: YD

256 Squadron
FB.VI 4.45 to 10.45
B.IX 3.45 to 8.45
NF.XII 5.43 to 9.43
NF.XIII 2.44 to 9.45
NF.XIX 9.45 to 9.46
Code: JT

264 Squadron
NF.II 5.42 to 1.44
FB.VI 7.43 to 10.43
NF.XIII 1.44 to 8.45
NF.30 11.45 to 7.46
NF.36 3.46 to 2.52
Code: PS

268 Squadron
FB.VI 9.45 to 3.46
Code: EG

KB424 was a Canadian-built Mosquito B.25 and when this view was made it was possibly serving with 162 Squadron. Martin Derry

58 Squadron's T.3 trainer, VT589/OT-Z, painted in the post-war yellow colour scheme adopted for these aircraft.
Tony Buttler Collection

305 (Polish) Squadron
FB.VI 12.43 to 11.46
Code: SM

307 (Polish) Squadron
NF.II 12.42 to 1.45
FB.VI 8.43 to 11.43
NF.XII 1.44 to 1.45
NF.30 10.44 to 11.46
Code: EW

333 (Norwegian) Squadron
NF.II 5.43 to 11.43
FB.VI 11.43 to 5.45
Code: KK (Norwegian control after 11.45)

334 (Norwegian) Squadron
FB.VI 5.45 to 3.52
Code: KK, F, RI (Norwegian control after 11.45)

400 Squadron RCAF
B.XVI 12.43 to 5.44
Code: None

404 Squadron RCAF
FB.VI 3.45 to 5.45
Code: EO

406 Squadron RCAF
PR.VIII and NF.XII 4.44 to 8.44
NF.30 7.44 to 8.45
Code: HU

409 Squadron RCAF
NF.XIII 3.44 to 7.45
Code: KP

410 Squadron RCAF
NF.II 11.42 to 12.43
NF.XIII 12.43 to 8.44
NF.30 8.44 to 6.45
Code: RA

418 Squadron RCAF
NF.II 3.43 to 9.43
FB.VI 5.43 to 9.45
Code: TH

456 Squadron RAAF
NF.II 1.43 to 2.44
FB.VI 7.43 to 10.43
NF.XVII 2.44 to 2.45
NF.30 12.44 to 6.45
Code: RX

464 Squadron RAAF
FB.VI 8.43 to 9.45
Code: SB

487 Squadron RNZAF
FB.VI 8.43 to 9.45
Code: EG

488 Squadron RNZAF
NF.XII 8.43 to 5.44
NF.XIII 10.43 to 9.44
NF.30 9.44 to 4.45
Code: ME

489 Squadron RNZAF
FB.VI 6.45 to 8.45
Code: P6

500 Squadron
NF.XIX and NF.30 4.47 to 10.48
Code: RAA

502 Squadron
B.25 7.46 to 12.47
NF.30 12.47 to 6.48
Code: RAC

504 Squadron
T.III 10.46 to 7.48
NF.30 5.47 to 7.48
Code: RAD

515 Squadron
NF.II 2.44 to 3.44
FB.VI 3.44 to 6.45
Code: 3P

521 Squadron
B.IV 8.42 to 3.43
Code: 50

527 Squadron
B.35 8.52 to 1.54
Code: WN

540 Squadron
B.IV 10.42 to 9.43
FB.VI 11.44 to 9.45
PR.VIII 12.42 to 9.43
B.IX 7.43 to 3.45
B.XVI 5.44 to 9.46
PR.32 11.44 to 11.45
PR.34 11.45 to 9.46, 12.47 to 12.52
Code: DH

543 Squadron
B.IV 6.43 to 10.43
Code: None

544 Squadron
B.IV 3.43 to 10.43
B.IX 10.43 to 3.45
B.XVI 4.44 to 10.45
PR.34 4.45 to 10.45
Code: None

571 Squadron
B.XVI 4.44 to 9.45
Code: 8K

600 Squadron
NF.XIX 1.45 to 8.45
Code: 6

604 Squadron
NF.XII 2.44 to 9.44
NF.XIII 4.44 to 4.45
Code: NG

605 Squadron
NF.II 2.43 to 7.43
FB.VI 7.43 to 8.45
NF.30 4.47 to 1.49
Code: UP, later RAL

608 Squadron
B.XX 8.44 to 4.45
B.XVI 3.45 to 8.45
B.25 10.44 to 4.45
NF.30 7.47 to 1.49
Code: 6T, later RAO

609 Squadron
NF.30 6.47 to 5.48
Code: RAP

613 Squadron
FB.VI 11.43 to 8.45
Code: SY

614 Squadron
B.25 6.45 to 7.45
Code: None

616 Squadron
T.III 10.46 to 1.48
NF.30 1.48 to 4.49
Code: RAW

617 Squadron
FB.VI 3.44 to late 1944(?)
Code: None

618 Squadron
B.IV 4.43 to 6.45
FB.VI 7.44 to 10.44, 3.45 to 6.45
B.XVI 10.44 to 6.45
Code: None

627 Squadron
B.IV 11.43 to 9.45
B.XVI 3.45 to 9.45
B.XX 7.44 to 9.45
B.25 10.44 to 9.45
Code: AZ

680 Squadron
B.IX 2.44 to 9.46
B.XVI 2.44 to 9.46
PR.34 3.46 to 9.46
Code: None

681 Squadron
B.IV 9.43 to 12.43
B.IX 9.43 to 12.43
Code: None

682 Squadron
B.IV 4.43 to 7.43
FB.VI 4.43 to 7.43
Code: None

683 Squadron
B.IV 5.43 to 6.43
FB.VI 5.43 to 6.43
Code: None

684 Squadron
NF.II 9.43 to 5.45
FB.VI 9.43 to 5.45
B.IX 10.43 to 5.45
B.XVI 2.44 to 2.46
PR.34 7.45 to 9.46
Code: None

692 Squadron
B.IV 1.44 to 6.44
B.XVI 3.44 to 9.45
Code: P3

Sea Mosquito TR.33 TW279 was coded 413/CW while serving with 790 NAS at Culdrose, Cornwall in the late 1940s. Martin Derry

A host of training, trials and other units also had Mosquitos on strength, sometimes in considerable numbers, often for support duties alongside other types. Besides frontline aircraft, many had examples of trainer variants.

1300 Met Flight (6.46 to 3.47), 1317 Training Flight (6.45 only), 1401 Met Flight, 1409 Met Flight (4.43 to 11.44), 1474 (Special Duties) Flight (12.42 to 1.43), 1692 (Radio Development) Flight - Code 4X (7.43 to 6.45)

6 Operational Training Unit (OTU), 8 OTU (Coastal 11.42 to 7.47), 13 OTU (1.44 to 5.47), 16 OTU (Fighter-Bomber + Bomber 12.44 to 3.48), 51 OTU (Night-Fighter 7.44 to 6.45), 54 OTU (Night-Fighter 8.44 to 5.47), 60 OTU (Night-Fighter + Fighter-Bomber 5.43 to 3.45), 132 OTU (5.44 to 12.44)

1653 Heavy Conversion Unit (HCU - Night-Fighter 3.46 to 12.48), 1655 (Mosquito) Conversion Unit (Bomber - 10.42 to 9.45), 1660 HCU - Code YW, 1672 (Mosquito) Conversion Unit (Fighter-Bomber - 2.44 to 8.45). 1692 (Bomber Support) Training Unit (6.44 to 6.45)

226 Operational Conversion Unit (OCU - Target towing 4.53 to 8.55), 228 OCU (Night Fighting 5.47 to 1954), 229 OCU (Target towing 12.54 to 6.56), 231 OCU (Bombing 5.47 to 1.50), 233 OCU (Target towing 6.55 to 8.56), 236 OCU (Target towing 9.52 to 9.54), 237 OCU - Code LP (Photo Reconnaissance 7.47 to 8.51), 238 OCU (Target towing 10.53 to 2.54)

204 Advanced Flying School (AFS) - Code FMO (to 1953)

Air Torpedo Development Unit (ATDU)

Aeroplane & Armament Experimental Establishment (A&AEE)

Armament Practice Station (APS - Target Towing 9.53 to 4.58)

Bomber Support Development Unit (BSDU 4.44 to 7.45)

Bombing Development Unit (BDU)

Bombing Trials Unit (BTU)

Central Bomber Establishment (CBE - 9.45 to 3.48)

Central Fighter Establishment (CFE)

Central Gunnery School (CGS)

Central Signals Establishment (CSE)

1 Civilian Anti-aircraft Co-operation Unit (CAACU 6.56 to 7.56), 3 CAACU (9.52 to 5.57), 3/4 CAACU (1.53 to 11.63), 5 CAACU (3.54 to 9.56)

Empire Test Pilots' School (ETPS)

Fighter Interception Unit (FIU) / Fighter Interception Development Unit (FIDU) - Code ZQ

Pathfinder Force Navigation Training Unit (PFNTU) - Code QF (1944 to 6.45)

1 Photographic Reconnaissance Unit (PRU) - Code LY (5.41 to 10.42)

Radio Warfare Establishment (RWE 7.45 to 9.46)

Royal Aircraft Establishment (RAE)

Signals Flying Unit (SFU)

Signals Intelligence Unit (SIU)

Telecommunications Flying Unit (TFU)

Royal Navy

811 Naval Air Squadron
FB.VI 9.45 to 8.46
TR.33 4.46 to 7.47
Mosquito Code FD4

RN Training and Second Line Squadrons (in some cases in small numbers as support equipment)

700 NAS
FB.VI 2.46 to 5.46

703 NAS
FB.VI 6.45 to 7.50
PR.XVI 9.47 to 6.48
TR.33 6.46 to 10.50
TR.37 12.48 to 5.50
TT.39 10.48

704 NAS (OTU for Mosquito Conversion)
T.III 10.45 to 12.45
FB.VI 4.45 to 7.45
B.25 1945 to 7.45
Code FD3

721 NAS
11.45 to 12.45

728 NAS Fleet Requirements Unit
T.III 10.45 to 6.46
PR.XVI 5.48 to 9.52
TT.39 3.49 to 5.52
Mosquito Codes M8 and HF

733 NAS Fleet Requirements Unit
B.25 11.45 to 12.45

751 NAS Radio Warfare Unit
FB.6 4.52 to 2.53
TR.33 3.52 to 6.53
PR.34 5.52 to 11.54

762 NAS Two Engine/Heavy Twin Conversion Unit
T.III 12.45 to 12.49
FB.6 8.45 to 11.49
TR.33 11.47 to 11.49
Codes FD6 and HA3

770 NAS Fleet Requirements Unit
PR.XVI 9.45 to 10.45
B.25 7.45 to 10.45

771 NAS Fleet Requirements Unit
FB.6 7.50 to 4.52
PR.16 12.48 to 8.52
B.25 8.45 to 5.47
PR.34 11.48 to 1.50
TR.33 5.47 to 3.50
TR.37 12.48 to 7.49
TT.39 1.50 to 1.52
Mosquito Codes GP8, FD and LP

772 NAS Fleet Requirements Unit
T.III 9.45
PR.XVI 10.45 to 11.46
B.25 5.45 to 8.46
PR.34 4.46 to 10.48
Mosquito Codes AR8 and AO

773 NAS Fleet Requirements Unit
FB.6 1.50 to 3.50

777 NAS Trials Unit
FB.VI 11.45 to 12.45
B.25 10.45 to 12.45

778 NAS Trials Unit
FB.VI 11.44 to 11.45
PR.16 12.46 to 9.47
B.25 5.45
TR.33 4.46 to 7.48
Mosquito Code FD

780 NAS Advanced Flying Training Unit
T.III 10.46 to 12.46
FB.VI 9.46 to 12.46

787 Air Fighting Development Squadron
FB.VI 12.46 to 5.48
TR.33 3.46 to 12.46

790 NAS
FB.6 7.46 to 12.48
B.25 10.46 to 2.48
TR.33 12.46 to 11.49
Mosquito Codes Z1, P0, P7, DL and CW

797 NAS Fleet Requirements Unit
B.25 7.45

DZ228/YP-D, an NF.II belonging to 23 Squadron, was photographed flying over Malta in February 1943. *Crown Copyright*

105 Squadron's DZ353/GB-E, a Mosquito B.IV bomber. *Crown Copyright*

RS709 was built as a B.35 bomber but eventually converted to TT.35 target tug format. It is seen here as '47' of 3/4 Civilian Anti-Aircraft Co-operation Unit (CAACU) at Exeter, in May 1961. *Martin Derry*

SERVICE OVER THE SEA

A Mosquito FB.VI of 143 Squadron and the Banff Strike Wing pictured during a mission. The serial is not visible but the aircraft carries eight underwing rockets.
Tony Buttler Collection

There was yet one further role in which the Mosquito performed superbly and where it would again become a feared adversary… this time over water. Here we examine the work of those Mosquitos that equipped RAF Coastal Command and a selection of the successes they recorded, especially against enemy shipping.

Early connections for the Mosquito with Coastal Command came during 1942 when 264 Squadron's fighters flew patrols across the Bay of Biscay to protect Coastal Command bombers from Luftwaffe interceptors. In early 1943 this unit also began to attack enemy ground and sea targets. Then in 1944 the FB.VI began to equip Coastal Command, with 248 Squadron as the first recipient. This

unit also received examples of the FB.XVIII 'Tsetse' Mosquitos armed with the heavy 57mm (6-pdr) gun and its Molins auto-load system. The new weapon had been tested initially using a damaged Mosquito fuselage and during offensive operations aircrews reported that, when the gun was fired, there was a clear cut but momentary retardation (negative acceleration or slowing-down). Nevertheless, the Mosquito's airframe absorbed the additional recoil and blast without trouble (nose machine guns were used to help aim the 57mm). A new 65gal fuel tank had also been installed inside the fuselage to extend the available flying time over the Bay of Biscay.

With the FB.VI as the unit's primary mount, 248 formed a special

detachment for its Mk.XVIIIs, which was active until early 1945; 254 Squadron would use the XVIII for a short time after that, but no squadron became fully equipped on this mark. The idea was to mix the two versions and, with underwing bombs carried as well, the XVIII was a powerful machine. Several U-boats were damaged by 'Tsetses', but the heavy defensive fire put up by the enemy during Coastal Command missions would account for Mosquitos of both marks being shot down.

The unit's first major action took place on March 10, 1944, when two of its XVIIIs damaged a destroyer and fired on a U-boat (and shot down a Junkers Ju 88 with machine gun fire), while four of the FB.VIs

brought down at least two more of the escorting Junkers Ju 88s. On D-Day, June 6, 1944, 248 Squadron flew sorties to protect the invasion fleet and other aircraft, and on June 22 the Squadron's FB.VIs took the 25lb depth charge on its first operational deployment. That same month another newly converted Coastal Command FB.VI unit, 235 Squadron, joined 248 on anti-shipping and anti-aircraft duties. However, as the Allied ground forces moved into and across France, shipping targets in the English Channel and in the Bay of Biscay became thin on the ground, so the two squadrons moved north to find new prey.

Banff Strike Wing

They moved to Banff in northern Scotland and, when joined by another Coastal Command Mosquito unit, 333 Squadron, would form the famous Banff Strike Wing. These units would operate with Bristol Beaufighter squadrons from Dallachy, and their areas of interest for potential targets were primarily along the Norwegian coast and into the Skagerrak and ▶▶

Rockets mounted on their rails on a 143 Squadron aircraft. Note the aerodynamic shape of the wing attachments. Crown Copyright

Coastal Command Mosquitos attack enemy shipping in Aalesund Harbour on March 17, 1945. The vessel caught under fire in this view has defensive gun emplacements on its stern, showing how dangerous these operations could be to attacking aircraft. Crown Copyright

Despite so few examples having been built, there appears to be an abundance of photos of the FB.XVIII 'Tsetse' Mosquito armed with an adapted six-pounder anti-tank gun underneath its nose. These views have been included because they also show in some detail D-Day stripes on a Mosquito, the aircraft being NT225. Crown Copyright

Kattegat sea areas between Denmark and Sweden, where shipping targets were still in plentiful supply. In 1940 Germany had occupied Norway, a vital move for the import by sea of key raw materials for German industry, such as iron ore from Sweden. But by autumn 1944 the enemy's merchant convoys were desperately trying to supply Germany with enough iron ore, pyrite and other essential commodities to help keep the nation's war effort going.

The wing's operations became combined efforts, with firstly the Norwegian 333 Squadron setting out on reconnaissance sorties as 'outriders' to find suitable targets (for example, ships in convoy or in harbour) - these aircraft would often also act as Pathfinders. In response Beaufighters from 144 and 404 Squadrons based at Dallachy would then strike and hopefully destroy the targets, while the Mosquitos would provide escort and attack the defensive gun positions.

Sorties from Banff began on September 2, 1944, and the first combined strike followed on September 14. Here, 25 FB.VIs and four FB.XVIIIs (from both 235 and 248) plus 19 Beaufighters attacked four merchant ships and their two auxiliary trawler escorts/flak ships off Kristiansand. As a result the merchant

Another 'Tsetse' presents an image of menace, though this view was made during a sortie to produce photos for recognition purposes. Crown Copyright

This Mosquito has just fired its outermost rockets in what appears to be a practice sortie. Crown Copyright

ships *Pompeji* and *Iris* (both of more than 2,500 tons displacement) were seriously damaged and the escort *Sulldorf* was sunk. Three more merchant ships and an escort were sent to the bottom at Egersund on October 9 by Beaufighters and Mosquitos, and on October 15 a tanker and an escort were sunk near Kristiansand South.

During October the Mosquitos began to use unguided rocket projectiles against ships, carried on four racks under each wing, which quickly proved effective. Indeed, it was realised that rocket projectiles were superior to the 57mm gun, and so all Mosquitos were soon equipped with the new weapon. Two forms were available, a solid 25lb armour-piercing

version or a semi-armour-piercing 60lb weapon with its own explosive warhead, though the latter presented problems because the debris from the resulting more powerful explosion could bring down its carrier aircraft. The Mosquitos would usually dive at their shipping targets at an angle of around 20° and fire their projectiles from about 600 yards, usually all ⊗

FB.VIs of 333 (Norwegian) Squadron fly in formation. Ian Thirsk Collection

eight in one go – though they could be released in pairs. In addition, the rocket rails were set at different angles to ensure some would hit the ship directly, while others would strike the water in front and then carry on beneath the surface to pierce the hull and hopefully start the vessel sinking.

The next squadron to convert to the FB.VI was 143 in October 1944, and this unit began operations with the other Strike Wing squadrons during the following month. The first combined operation to include 143 took place on November 13 when shipping was attacked off Egersund.

The biggest anti-shipping strike to date took place eight days later, and on December 26, aircraft from Banff and Dallachy damaged the *Cygnus* and *Tenerife* using rockets and 57mm gunfire. The *La France* and three other small merchant vessels had also been sunk by the end of December.

Some Mosquitos were lost during these operations, particularly so on January 15, 1945, when six were shot down... five by defending Focke-Wulf Fw 190 fighters. Further Coastal Command aircraft had been lost to enemy fighters a few days earlier, but on that occasion at least four enemy fighters were also brought down. From late 1944 the defensive Luftwaffe fighter strength had been increased and this began to take its toll on Strike Wing aircraft, so in response the North American P-51 Mustangs of 315 (Polish) Squadron were moved to Peterhead to fly escort whenever this was possible.

The Strike Wing operation staged on January 15 had been to Leirvik harbour in an attempt to destroy the 5,165-ton merchant ship *Claus Rickmers*, loaded with a suspected cargo of 'heavy water' (deuterium

On August, 12, 1944, a German 'M' Class minesweeper and two trawler-type auxiliaries come under attack by FB.VIs belonging to 248 Squadron, in the mouth of the Gironde River, off Royan, France. Key Collection

COMBAT
M A C H I N E S

Here FB.VI RS625/NE-D of
143 Squadron has been fitted
with long-range tanks where
the innermost pairs of rocket
projectiles would usually be.
Tony Buttler Collection

the Germans were transporting
complete Wehrmacht divisions by
sea through the Kattegat to help
defend Germany against the ever
closing Allied offensive, so Mosquitos
were accordingly fitted with 100gal
drop tanks to increase their range
to attack these movements, and to
reach targets even further east as far
as Oslo Fjord. On March 7 no fewer
than 34 Mosquitos hit a convoy of
fully-loaded tank landing craft, five
of which were sunk. Then on the
17th, 31 aircraft from 235 and 248
Squadrons attacked traffic around
Aalesund where they despatched one
ship of 3,000 tons and two smaller
vessels. Here the shore flak was
intense and two Mosquitos did not
get home.

On March 25 the wing attacked a
6,000-ton tanker in Norangsfjord
and in the ensuing air battle against
more than 30 Luftwaffe fighters
the Mosquitos claimed three of
the five enemy aircraft shot down.
The final strike in March, involving
44 Mosquitos, resulted in the
sinking of two more ships and
the *Scharhorn* (2,643 tons) seriously
damaged. By early April 404

oxide) used in the German nuclear
bomb programme. The German
fighters attacked the Mosquitos as
they broke away from their strike
runs and the outcome was one of the
biggest air battles to take place thus
far over Norway. The *Claus Rickmers*
was attacked again on the 17th and
was left in a badly damaged state.
Shortly afterwards 248 Squadron
relinquished its Tsetse Mosquitos, and
while on another shipping raid, this
time over Midgulen Fjord, delayed-
action bombs were released over its
high cliffs.

A Busy Spring
Poor weather disrupted the flow
of combat sorties during January
and well into February, though
on February 21 Mosquitos sank
one merchant vessel and seriously
damaged two more near Leirvik. But
March brought excellent weather
conditions and the campaign was
resumed in earnest with plenty
of available targets; the wing
became busier than ever, though
still with losses of its own. By then

Brrrr! Ice is swept off the wings
of a 235 Squadron FB.VI at Banff
in 1944. Ian Thirsk Collection

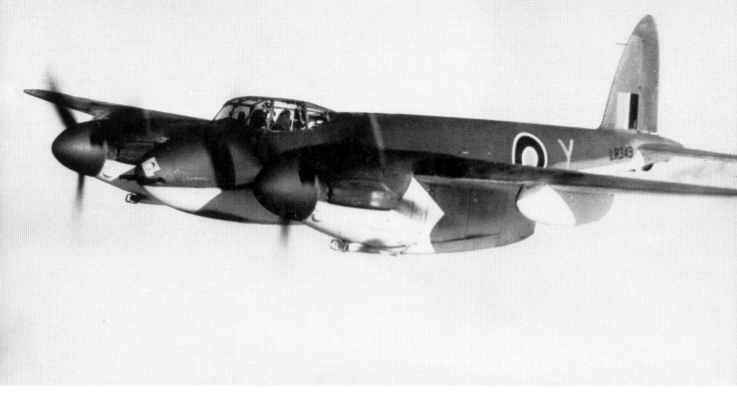

Squadron (RCAF) had relinquished its Beaufighters and it began flying from Banff as the wing's fifth Mosquito unit, along with 143, 235, 248 and 333 (Norwegian) Squadrons.

April opened with an attack by 31 Mosquitos against Sandefjord, at this time being used to evacuate German troops. The *Concordia* (5,100 tons) and *William Blumer* (3,600 tons) were both sunk and other large vessels damaged.

By then the German Navy's U-boats had been withdrawn from their French bases back to Germany and to Scandinavia, so they too were

passing through this area trying to reach the Atlantic. This resulted in one of the wing's most successful operations when, on April 9, it found and attacked a convoy comprising a German 'M' Class minesweeper leading four U-boats, all sailing on the surface. Two submarines, U-804 and U-1065, were hit in the first pass and both were sunk, though as one settled by the stern it blew up and the resulting debris brought down an RAF Film Unit Mosquito and killed its crew. Shortly afterwards U-843 was also sent to the bottom, in this case by a single Mosquito

flown by Fg Off A J Rendall.

Two days later, in the next major operation, 35 Mosquitos were accompanied by 12 Mustangs during a raid on Porsgrunn Fjord. Two Mosquitos did not return (although one was able to crash-land in Sweden) but in this successful mission four more merchant vessels were sunk (three Norwegian and one German, the *Kalmar*) plus another two damaged. As on the 9th, a very similar situation with U-boats arose on the 19th when another force of Mosquitos flying over the Kattegat, and escorted by Mustangs, spotted four more surfaced submarines sailing in line astern behind another 'M' Class minesweeper. Rocket projectiles fired by the Mosquitos approaching in a shallow dive sent U-251 to the bottom, while U-2335 was extensively damaged. This time two Mosquitos had to make forced landings after being damaged by flak, one of them again in Sweden but the other reached Denmark.

Silver lining

An attack of an altogether different kind took place two days later on April 21. Another large-scale anti-shipping patrol by the Banff Strike Wing had been aborted because of very poor visibility over the Kattegat, but on the way home (and just after the 24-strong Mustang escort had been released to return to its base),

the wing accidently discovered a
force of German raiders hugging
the waves about 150 miles from the
Scottish coast. No fewer than 42
Mosquitos piled in on the enemy

aircraft, comprising 18 Junkers Ju
88s and Heinkel He 111s all carrying
torpedoes, which were not aware
that they had been spotted. In all nine
enemy aircraft were shot down, most

of the remainder were damaged, and
with no loss to the Mosquitos.

Unlike in other theatres in the
European war, the Banff Strike
Wing was busy right until the end.
A small coastal U-boat sailing in the
Kattegat, U-2359, succumbed on
May 2 to an attack by 35 Mosquitos
using rocket projectiles, and another
was damaged. Finally, on May 4 a
force of 40 Mosquitos, taken from
all five squadrons, spotted a convoy
that included two large merchant
ships, a flak vessel and a frigate,
sailing to the north of Aarhus in
the Kattegat. Using their firepower
the Mosquitos sent three escorts
(including the flak ship) and the
3,000-ton *Wolfgang* to the bottom,
while the second large ship and
two further escorts were all badly
damaged. This operation included
Mosquitos from 404 Squadron on this
unit's second and final large outing,
a total of 18 Mustangs (from 19 and
234 Squadrons) flew as the escort
and, as with some previous attacks,
a small number of Vickers Warwicks
provided air-sea rescue facilities for
any Allied aircraft having to ditch.

Just four days later VE Day signalled
the end of the war in Europe. But
that was not quite the end for the
Banff Strike Wing, because as late as
May 21 both 143 and 248 Squadrons
were still flying sorties searching for
U-boats, which it was thought might
not yet have learnt that the war

One of the B.XVI Mosquitos allocated for trials with special RAE Farnborough/Vickers rocket-powered models is pictured with an example in position underneath its fuselage. *National Archives*

operations could be spectacular, but were dangerous for the Mosquito crews and one imagines quite horrific for the crews of the ships under attack from rockets, bombs and cannon. But once again the Mosquito's versatility had been shown to the full. Although Mosquito crews suffered considerable losses (and not just in the Banff Strike Wing, but of course in some of the other theatres worldwide where the type operated), their skill and courage had done so much to help bring the war to an end.

Experimental

Post-war a few research and experimental roles were found for the Mosquito. Perhaps the highest profile task (and one which keeps to the 'over-water' element of this section) was the carriage and release of unmanned Vickers supersonic flying models off the Scilly Isles in 1947-48. Three Mosquito B.XVIs were involved in the drop trials, serials PF543 , PF604 and ML966, all flying out of St Eval in Cornwall. The rocket-powered test vehicles were released at around 35,000ft altitude over the sea near the island of St Mary's and on October 9, 1948, one of them recorded a maximum speed of Mach 1.38, thereby becoming the UK's second supersonic flying machine following another de Havilland product, the DH.108 research aircraft.

had ended. However, 404 Squadron was disbanded on May 25, while 143 disbanded and then reformed on that same day as 14 Squadron.

It should not be forgotten that throughout the period covered in this section the Banff Strike Wing was supported in its anti-shipping role by Bristol Beaufighters of the North Coates Wing in Lincolnshire, and by those based at Dallachy in Scotland. Throughout the period of the Strike Wing's existence, RAF Banff itself was commanded by Gp Capt the Honourable J W 'Max' Aitken. Wg Cdr G D 'Bill' Sise from New Zealand commanded 248 for a long period, to become the wing's most experienced

commander until he was rested in February 1945. Australian Wg Cdr R A Atkinson was CO for 235 until killed in December 1944 and replaced by Wg Cdr A H Simmonds, while 143 was commanded by Wg Cdr E H McHardy. He was succeeded as CO 143 by Wg Cdr Maurice - in fact an alias for Max Guedj, a famous Jewish Free French pilot flying with the RAF. Guedj was shot down and killed during the Leirvik missions in mid-January 1945 and was replaced by Wg Cdr Christopher Foxley-Norris who led the squadron, and the Banff Strike Wing, until the end of the war.

These Coastal Command strike

A rare air-to-air photo of an unidentified 404 Squadron Mosquito FB.VI, again taken in April 1945. Just two rockets are loaded under the port wing. *Graham Pitchfork Collection*

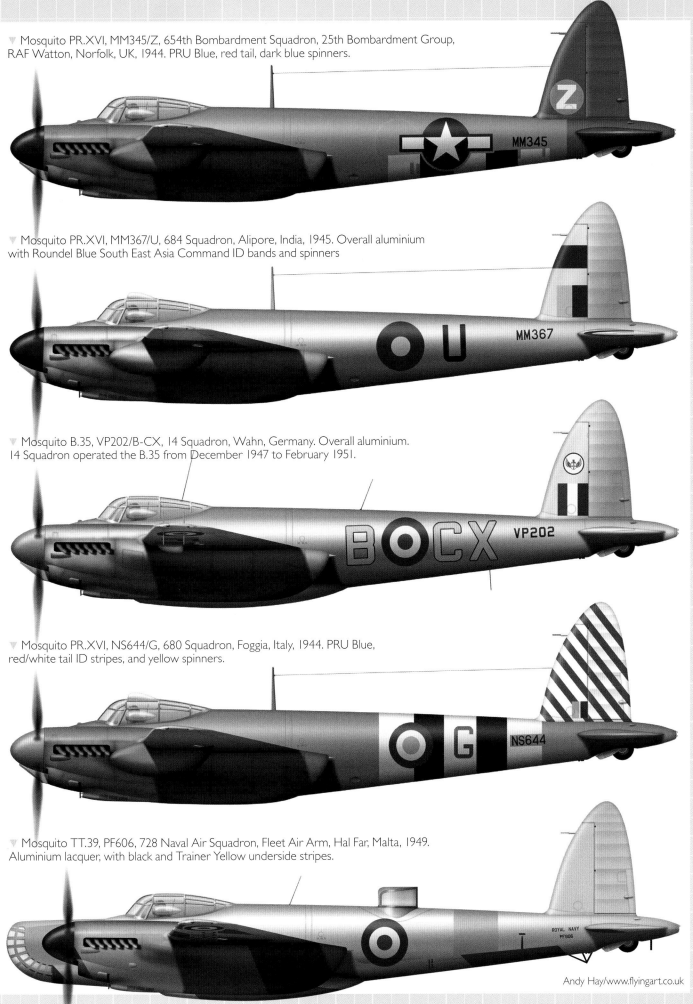

▼ Mosquito PR.XVI, MM345/Z, 654th Bombardment Squadron, 25th Bombardment Group,
RAF Watton, Norfolk, UK, 1944. PRU Blue, red tail, dark blue spinners.

▼ Mosquito PR.XVI, MM367/U, 684 Squadron, Alipore, India, 1945. Overall aluminium
with Roundel Blue South East Asia Command ID bands and spinners

▼ Mosquito B.35, VP202/B-CX, 14 Squadron, Wahn, Germany. Overall aluminium.
14 Squadron operated the B.35 from December 1947 to February 1951.

▼ Mosquito PR.XVI, NS644/G, 680 Squadron, Foggia, Italy, 1944. PRU Blue,
red/white tail ID stripes, and yellow spinners.

▼ Mosquito TT.39, PF606, 728 Naval Air Squadron, Fleet Air Arm, Hal Far, Malta, 1949.
Aluminium lacquer, with black and Trainer Yellow underside stripes.

Andy Hay/www.flyingart.co.uk

OVERSEAS 'MOSSIES'

Mosquito A52-500/NA-A of 1 Squadron RAAF was an FB.VI supplied directly from the UK. The roundels denote service with South East Asia Command. Tony Buttler Collection

With so many Mosquitos delivered it was no surprise that numerous air arms beyond Britain's shores would acquire the type. This section provides details for these purchases and acquisitions, including aircraft flown by Commonwealth countries based 'at home' and operated under their own control. Note: sources providing information on numbers delivered to different air arms vary considerably, but this section has been checked by expert Ian Thirsk and is accurate.

Australia

To go with the home-built examples detailed in this publication's 'gun nose' section, de Havilland also supplied another 46 Mosquito FB.VIs and 29 PR.XVIs to Australia which received the serials A52-500 onwards. During the war, 14 T.IIIs were supplied in kit form, which became A52-1002 to A52-1015. The type served well into the 1950s and the home units were as follows (with dates when Mosquitos were on strength).

- 1 Squadron (code NA) 1.45 to 8.46
- 87 Squadron (code SU) 9.44 to 7.46 and 3.48 to 12.53
- 94 Squadron (code OB) 5.45 to 1.46
- 1 PRU
- 5 OTU – 11.43 to 1945

Belgium

In 1947 the Belgian Air Force ordered 24 NF.30s, which would carry serials MB-1 to MB-24. These were followed by seven late-production T.3s converted to TT.3 target-tugs as MA-1 to MA-7, and then in October 1951 by three FB.VIs converted by Fairey at Ringway in Manchester to TT.6 target-tugs (as MC-1 to MC-3). The NF.30s served with 10 and 11 Squadrons within the air force's 1 Wing.

- 10 Squadron (code ND) 5.48 to mid-1956
- 11 Squadron (code KT) 11.51 to mid-1952
- 600 TT (Target Tug) Flight (code B2) 3.47 onwards

Canada

During 1945 the Royal Canadian Air Force had two squadrons with Mosquitos on strength.

- 13 Squadron (B.25s) - 4.45 to 7.45
- 133 Squadron (FB.26s) - 4.45 to 9.45

China

In what was to become the biggest overseas operator of Mosquitos, the Chinese Nationalist Air Forces ordered more than 200 from Canada, mostly FB.26s but with a small number of T.27s. The first aircraft arrived in 1948 but during their delivery voyage some of these aircraft suffered airframe deterioration and hence never entered service. Those that did flew with 1, 3 and 4 Squadrons and were mostly flown in combat during the Civil War against the Communists, five apparently being captured by the Chinese People's Liberation Army.

Czechoslovakia

When the Czechoslovak Air Force was re-constituted in 1945 the organisation of its units reverted back to pre-1938 consensus, so the term 'Squadron' was dropped and the old Air Regiments returned. In January 1946, 311 (Czech) Squadron RAF was disbanded and immediately re-constituted as 6 letecká divize (6th Air Division), comprising Letecký pluk 24 and Letecký pluk 25 (24th and 25th Air Regiments). From 1947, 26 FB.VIs went to Czechoslovakia as B-36s where they were assigned to Letecký pluk 24, to equip a headquarters flight, 1st Squadron (1.letka) and 2nd Squadron (2.letka). Two (possibly three) trainer T.IIIs (CB-36s) were also supplied. Letecký pluk 24 was disbanded in 1949 though a small number of Mosquitos continued flying. The final example was struck off charge in 1951.

Dominica

From 1948 the Dominican Republic Air Force acquired six FB.VIs and three T.29s from Canada. These served with the Escuadrón de Caza Bombardeos from August 1948 until July 1954.

Belgian NF.30 MB11 (NT377)/KT-O of 11 Squadron at Beauvechain in 1951. Ian Thirsk Collection

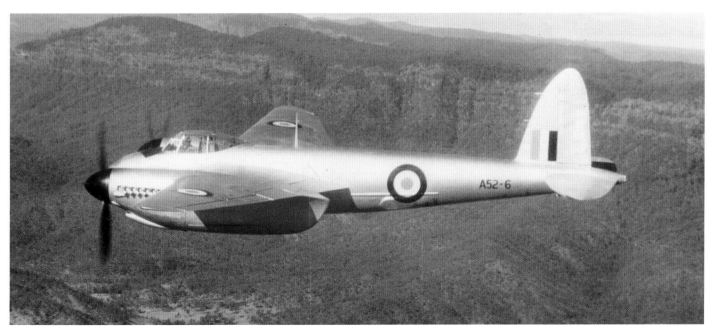

This Australian Mosquito PR.40, RAAF serialled A52-6, carries post-war roundels. BAE Heritage Collection

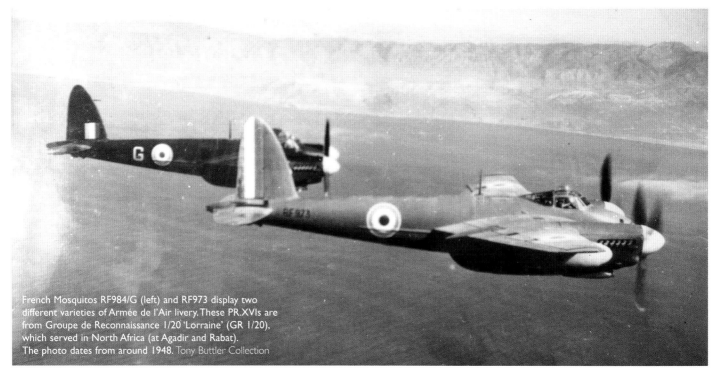

French Mosquitos RF984/G (left) and RF973 display two different varieties of Armée de l'Air livery. These PR.XVIs are from Groupe de Reconnaissance 1/20 'Lorraine' (GR 1/20), which served in North Africa (at Agadir and Rabat). The photo dates from around 1948. Tony Buttler Collection

France

The biggest user of Mosquitos in Europe, outside of the UK, was to be France's Armée de l'Air. The first machines were delivered during 1945 and the final number supplied was 194, comprising 112 FB.VIs, 38 PR.XVIs, 12 T.3s and 32 NF.30s . In November 1945 Groupe de Chasse (Fighter Group or Fighter Wing) GC 1/3 formed on the FB.VI and was quickly followed by a second FB.VI unit, GC 3/5. The PR.XVIs and NF.30s were flown by Groupe de Reconnaissance (Reconnaissance Group) GR 1/20, with some specialisation in night-fighting; by October 1949 this unit, then called GR 1/31, had become a mixed recce and night-fighter group.

All these Mosquitos wore their original RAF serials during Armée de l'Air service. From January 1947 FB.VIs operated in French Indo-

This Israeli Mosquito TR.33 was photographed at Gatwick, UK during its delivery flight. Serial '4x3186' (for what is ex-TW238) was an unofficial 'quasi-civil' registration. Tony Buttler Collection

China (later Vietnam) and became heavily involved in operations against opposing Communist forces. The FB.VI was withdrawn from French service in 1949 but the NF.30 and PR.XVI flew until June 1953.
• GC 1/3 'Corse' (from November 1946 GC 1/6) – 11.45 to 10.49
• GC 3/5 'Normandie-Niemen' (from 1947 GC 2/6) – 11.45 to Nov 1949
• GR 1/20 'Lorraine' (from 1947 GMRCN 1/31) – 11.45 to 7.53

Israel

The first Mosquito, PR.16 NS811, reached Israel in 1948 and flew initially with the serial D-160 and then 2101. A second example, 2102, never flew, and the major buy was to be 62 ex-French Armée de l'Air aircraft (ie then third-hand) acquired in 1951. Needing extensive refurbishment, these FB.6s, NF.30s, PR.16s and

T.3s were numbered 2103 to 2164. Further examples (FB.6s, de-navalised TR.33s and PR.16s) were later purchased in Britain from store and numbered 2165 to 2184 and 2190 to 2192. Initially these aircraft were used for reconnaissance and border patrol flights, but in the Sinai (Suez) Campaign starting on October 29, 1956, they flew ground attack and strafing operations against Egyptian troops and facilities, using bombs and rockets. The survivors were retired in 1958.
• 103 Squadron – 6.48 onwards
• 109 Squadron – 2.52 to 5.56
• 110 Squadron – 8.53 to 10.55, 10.56 to 1.57
• 115 Squadron – 6.56 to 1.57

New Zealand

A large quantity of Mosquitos were supplied to the Royal New Zealand Air Force to equip home-based units. The total embraced 76 FB.VIs and four T.IIIs plus an FB.40 and four T.43s; however the FB.40 was transferred following a landing accident in New Zealand and it was never repaired.
• 14 Squadron (Training) 1.49 to 9.51
• 75 Squadron (code YC) 11.46 to 4.52

Norway

In June 1945 RAF 333 and 334 (Norwegian) Squadrons returned home from their wartime service and then passed to Royal Norwegian Air Force control in November,

though by then just 334 still operated Mosquitos – 18 FB.VIs and five T.IIIs. A further 24 FB.VIs were supplied in 1947. Some had radar fitted to become 'temporary' night-fighters, but in 1951 the entire fleet was grounded following a fatal accident and the type was withdrawn entirely by 1952. Some FB.VIs exported to Norway had four-bladed propellers.

• 334 Squadron (code AK) 5.45 to 3.52

South Africa
In all, two F.IIs, four FB.VIs, 18 PR.IXs plus 30 PR.XVIs were supplied to the South African Air Force.

• 60 Squadron (code JS) 2.43 to 8.45 and 1.49 to 12.50

Soviet Union
The USSR acquired ex-105 Squadron DK296, a B.IV Series II, for evaluation

NF.XIXs in total were despatched, with deliveries starting in July 1948… but beforehand the original three-bladed propellers were replaced by four-bladed units. The Swedish Air Force designation was J 30, the aircraft carried serials from 30001-30060 and they equipped F 1 Fighter Wing. All

had been withdrawn by March 1955 when the last J 30 flight was made.

• Flottiljer F.1 – 6.48 to 6.53

Switzerland
Switzerland acquired two Mosquitos during World War Two through forced-landings on its territory. ▶▶

Royal Norwegian Air Force AK-F of 334 Squadron pictured in June 1949. The serial of this FB.VI, RS650, is written in small lettering on the forward part of the fin, except that 'RS650' had been applied incorrectly since this was actually RS605. *Key Collection*

by the Soviet Aircraft Research Institute. Serious thought went towards licence manufacture of the Mosquito but this was eventually rejected. DK296 was wrecked in a crash on its ninth flight.

Sweden
Refurbished Mosquitos were ordered by Sweden in 1948 from surplus stocks held by the British Ministry of Supply. More than half had apparently never been in service, and prior to this purchase the Swedish Air Force had no night-fighter capability. Sixty

New Zealand T.43 NZ2306 of 75 Squadron pictured at Ohakea. *Royal New Zealand Air Force*

When PR.IV DK310 of 1 PRU 'arrived' on September 24, 1942, it was the first Mosquito to come into 'non-Allied' hands. This prompted the UK to make an agreement with Switzerland, in August 1943, for its air arm to use this particular aircraft, initially with serial E-42 though by 1945 it was carrying mail and so had the civil registration HB-IMO. It was withdrawn in August 1946. On September 30, 1944, 515 Squadron's FB.VI NS993 made a forced landing and it too would subsequently serve with the Swiss Air Force, in this case on research work with a jet engine installed beneath its fuselage.

Turkey

Altogether 96 FB.VIs and ten T.IIIs were delivered to Turkey from 1947 with the latter redesignated T.III(T) as torpedo-bombers. Supplied by Fairey at Ringway from surplus RAF stock (the T.IIIs were all new-build examples), by April 1948 they had equipped three regiments, the first of which was the 3rd Regiment in the anti-shipping role. After the 3rd Regiment had been disbanded, 1st and 2nd Regiments were redesignated 1st and 2nd Air Base and Mosquitos were flown until 1953-54.

- 1st Regiment (subsequently 1st Air Base) 1947 to 1954
- 2nd Regiment (subsequently 2nd Air Base) 1947 to 1954
- 3rd Regiment – 1947 to 1950-51

United States

Around 200 Mosquitos joined the USAAF. In 1943, 40 Canadian-built airframes (34 B.XXs and six B.VIIs) were modified by Bell Aircraft into reconnaissance F-8-DHs with the serials 43-34924 to 43-34963. Sixteen went to Europe while possibly as many as another 160 Hatfield-built photo-reconnaissance PR.XVIs (certainly 145) joined the US Eighth Air Force from February 1944 (these retained their RAF serials). From August 1944 the 25th Bombardment Group in Europe used them to fly photographic and mapping missions over enemy territory, day and night. A few examples with the 654th Bombardment Squadron had wire recording equipment to enable them to perform 'Red Stocking' missions… collecting messages from Allied agents in enemy territory (these sorties needed to be flown above 30,000ft to enable them to hear the agent's signals). A batch of NF.30s also equipped the 416th Night Fighter Squadron in Italy.

- 416th Night Fighter Squadron – 11.44 to 6.45
- 425th Night Fighter Squadron – Spring 1945 to mid-1945
- 653rd Bombardment (Weather Reconnaissance) Squadron – 4.44 to 4.45
- 654th Bombardment Squadron – 4.44 to 4.45
- 802nd Reconnaissance Group: 8th Reconnaissance Squadron (later 25th Bombardment Group [Reconnaissance]); later 492nd Bombardment Group –4.44 to 8.44

Yugoslavia

A total of 140 Mosquitos – 76 FB.VIs, 60 NF.38s and four T.IIIs, were delivered to the Yugoslav Air Force (Jugoslovensko ratno vazduho-plovstyo or JRV) from autumn 1951 onwards. The first examples went to the 103rd Reconnaissance Regiment (a training and conversion unit), then in 1952 FB.VIs equipped 32 Bomber Division, 184 Reconnaissance Regiment (assigned to 3rd Aviation Corps) and 97 Aviation Regiment (an element of 21st Mixed Aviation Division supporting the navy). Several of those with the 32nd Bombardment Division and 21st Mixed Aviation Division were adapted to carry torpedoes, others had cameras installed, and then in 1953-54 six FB.VIs were converted to T.III trainers. After the Soviet intervention in Hungary during 1956, Mosquito FB.VIs from the 32nd and 184th patrolled the Hungary-Yugoslav border. Most Mosquitos had been withdrawn from service by mid-1960, although a handful of FB.VIs modified as target-tugs stayed in use with a sea-reconnaissance squadron and with the anti-aircraft school until 1963.

- 32nd Bomber Aviation Division –1952 to c12.56
- 97th Aviation Regiment – 1952 to 1959
- 103rd Reconnaissance Aviation Regiment – 1951 to c12.54
- 184th Reconnaissance Aviation Regiment – 1952 to mid-1960

Switzerland did not order Mosquitos but acquired two aiframes. This FB.VI, ex-NS993 of 515 Squadron, tested the home-grown SM-1 jet engine.... a development of the Armstrong Siddeley Mamba turboprop, with propeller gear removed and replaced by a compressor, and designed to power the N-20 Aiguillon fighter. Key Collection

This JRV NF.38 is serial '8030', ex-RAF VT696. Ian Thirsk Collection

One of the 40 F-8/B.XXs supplied to the USAAF from Canada, pictured (it is thought) in 1945. NACA

ROOFTOP FURY

P ossessing excellent all-round performance, the Mosquito became a workhorse for many diverse tasks during World War Two. One of these was low-flying daytime pin-point attacks against specific targets in Occupied Europe. The type's excellent speed and handling at low altitude, together with its ability to carry a useful bomb load over considerable distances, made it the ideal fighter-bomber for just this sort of high-value targeting. Indeed, the Mosquito proved to be a far better and more powerful warplane than the aircraft types it replaced in this role, notably the Bristol Blenheim.

Percy 'Pick' Pickard (centre) was involved in various special duties activities during the war, one of these being his assignment to 161 Squadron. Here he is photographed with one of the unit's Westland Lysander aircraft, with the well-known special operations pilot Hugh Verity, seen second from left.
Malcolm V Lowe Collection

Initial attacks

The announced existence to the British public of the Mosquito in RAF service first came about due to a daring low-altitude daylight raid carried out by four Mosquito Mk.IV bombers of 105 Squadron. Flying from RAF Leuchars in Fife, Scotland, the Mosquitos attacked the Gestapo headquarters in Oslo, Norway, on September 25, 1942. The raid tragically failed in its main objective and several Norwegian civilians were killed – underlining the danger of making pin-point attacks on small high-value targets in built-up areas. One of the Mosquitos was also lost.

The Mosquito took part in some of the most audacious low-level daylight precision strikes of World War Two, as **Malcolm V Lowe** explains

Several weeks later, a further early pin-point bombing mission in which Mosquitos were involved was the December 6, 1942 raid on the Philips electronics factory at Eindhoven in the Netherlands (Operation Oyster). This was carried out by units of 2 Group, Bomber Command, but only comprised a small number of Mosquito Mk.IV bombers from 105 and 139 Squadrons. The main part of the strike force comprised RAF-operated Douglas Bostons and Lockheed Venturas. The relative vulnerability of the attackers was reflected by the comparatively high losses on the raid, at least 14 of the bombers (but just one Mosquito) being shot down with many others damaged. However, this and other sorties at low-level on specific targets did prove the validity and value of such strikes… but clearly a fast, powerful and hard-hitting machine was needed, rather than the decidedly pedestrian Bostons and Venturas. Mosquito provided the answer.

Low-level specialist

The Mosquito version of choice for pin-point precision attack operations was the highly capable FB.Mk.VI, 'FB' standing for 'fighter-bomber'. Powered by two Rolls-Royce Merlin 25 engines of 1,635hp each at 2,250ft with a single-stage, two speed supercharger, this mark introduced a modified wing, which was re-stressed and reinforced to carry a single 250lb or 500lb bomb beneath each outer mainplane section on a streamlined ordnance pylon. It was armed with four 20mm Hispano cannon in the lower forward fuselage, and four .303in Browning machine guns in the nose/forward fuselage. The rear part of the bomb bay could carry two 250lb or 500lb bombs.

The initial development aircraft flew in June 1942. During service testing carried out by the Aeroplane and Armament Experimental Establishment (A&AEE) at Boscombe Down, the type's maximum speed at low level was clocked at 384mph. In total, some 2,298 FB.VIs were built.

Evolving capability

Although the FB.VI was subsequently widely used by RAF squadrons and eventually became a stalwart in the 2nd Tactical Air Force (2nd TAF), ⧫⧫

One of the Mosquito units that became adept at the specialist role of daylight pin-point attacks was 487 Squadron, RNZAF. Several of the unit's Mosquito FB.VIs posed for this formation photograph, wearing the squadron's famous 'EG' code with MM417/EG-T nearest. JB via Malcolm V Lowe

A rearwards-looking strike camera caught a moment from the famous Amiens prison raid in February 1944, with the gaol on the left having taken a hit, and a second low-flying Mosquito visible at the top left of the image. JB via Malcolm V Lowe

This low-level recce photo taken three days after the raid graphically illustrated the damage inflicted on Amiens gaol, and the highly-visible breach in the prison's outer wall. The 'hole' allowed a number of important prisoners to escape, although many were later re-captured. Malcolm V Lowe Collection

The aftermath of the Operation Jericho Amiens prison raid is visible in this photograph showing the damaged outer wall. The structure still stands, although was subsequently re-built. Malcolm V Lowe Collection

several units specifically evolved as experts in the specialised task of delivering ordnance onto pin-point targets at low level. In particular, 140 Wing of 2nd TAF was at the forefront of these operations. It comprised 21 Squadron RAF, 464 Royal Australian Air Force (RAAF) Squadron, and 487 Royal New Zealand Air Force (RNZAF) Squadron.

It was these three units that participated in the first significant high-profile precision assault, which also gained headlines worldwide. The attack was the famous Amiens prison raid (Operation Jericho) of February 18, 1944. Although the expressed purpose of this mission was to liberate French resistance personnel and other prisoners held at the gaol, there has been controversy in more recent times as to the actual intentions of the raid and the story 'behind the scenes'. Nevertheless, there can be no doubting the remarkable airmanship displayed by those involved.

There was considerable pre-attack planning for the raid, even including the construction of a special scale model of the prison for aircrews to study. A large amount of intelligence was known about the gaol and its surroundings, with French resistance operatives in the vicinity providing vital information.

The daylight raid itself comprised the three squadrons from 140

The Aarhus attack of October 1944 was one of the most important Mosquito daylight rooftop raids. Several Mosquitos are visible in this image, making their bomb runs as photographed from a Mosquito flying ahead of them. Malcolm V Lowe Collection

The classic mark of Mosquito for long-range daylight strikes against pin-point targets was the FB.VI, as shown here by MM417/EG-T from one of the precision attack units, 487 Squadron, RNZAF. Bombs could be carried externally under the wings additional to inside the bomb bay. Malcolm V Lowe Collection

Wing based at RAF Hunsdon in Hertfordshire, while a specialist camera-carrying Mosquito (from the RAF's Film Production Unit – FPU) also accompanied the raid. The dramatic imagery made during the mission subsequently proved to be a propaganda coup for the Allies.

Gp Capt Percy Pickard, RAF Hunsdon's 140 Wing 'boss', was placed in overall leadership of the mission, although he had just limited experience of low-level attacks of this nature. The Mosquitos were delegated an escort provided by several squadrons of RAF Hawker Typhoons, which were far from ideal covering fighters… but were the best available in numbers at that time. They included 174 Squadron from RAF Westhampnett in Sussex, and 198 Squadron based at RAF Manston, Kent.

The actual attack was carried out by 464 and 487 Squadrons at rooftop level, with 21 Squadron aircraft in reserve. It was an outstanding success. The prison was hit several times, killing numerous German personnel although tragically some of the French prisoners also died. Many more managed to escape through a major breach in the gaol's high outer wall.

Sadly, Pickard did not return from the raid. His Mosquito was shot down by the Focke-Wulf Fw 190A fighter flown by Wilhelm Mayer of JG 26 (Jagdgeschwader – fighter wing). Pickard and his navigator, Flt Lt John

Alan Broadley were killed. Several Fw 190s of JG 26 intercepted the raid and a number of air battles ensued between them and the covering Typhoons, two of which were lost. Also failing to return was a second Mosquito, flown by Sq Ldr A I McRitchie.

Pickard's loss was a particular blow to the RAF. He was a well-known character for his wartime exploits, which had included several specialist operations completely separate to Mosquito sorties. This included his role in the Bruneval Raid of February 1942, and he had later been assigned to 161 Squadron and its clandestine operations in support

of the French resistance.

For the Bruneval Raid he was commander of 51 Squadron, whose Armstrong Whitworth Whitleys had dropped members of the 2nd Parachute Battalion in the vicinity of a German Würzburg radar site at Bruneval near Le Havre in northern France (Operation Biting), to seize components of the installation and then evacuate them by sea. After this he had flown daring sorties while assigned to 161 Squadron at RAF Tempsford, Bedfordshire, flying Westland Lysanders into Occupied France at night to drop off or pick up agents of the Special Operations Executive. ⟫

The Mosquitos of 140 Wing were certainly 'Gestapo hunters', targeting that organisation's infrastructure several times from rooftop height later in the war. This damage was inflicted during the October 1944 Aarhus raid. Malcolm V Lowe Collection

The low-level nature of the Mosquito raids is exemplified in this photograph taken during the attack on the Shellhus in Copenhagen, on March 21, 1945. A Mosquito can be seen in the left of the image at rooftop height, banking in the area of the target. JB via Malcolm V Lowe

Further success

The Amiens raid set the standard for additional precision strikes in the months following this extraordinary exploit. The experience gained from the mission proved invaluable, and a number of pin-point attacks were subsequently carried out against Gestapo and other high-profile and significant targets. Unlike the Philips raid of December 1942, the Amiens assault taught that attacks at ultra-low level, what came to be known as 'rooftop height', were possible but also dangerous for all involved, in the air and on the ground.

Several weeks after Amiens, on April 11, 1944 following a request by the Dutch resistance, six Mosquito FB.VIs of 613 (City of Manchester)

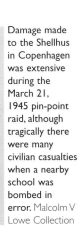

Damage made to the Shellhus in Copenhagen was extensive during the March 21, 1945 pin-point raid, although tragically there were many civilian casualties when a nearby school was bombed in error. Malcolm V Lowe Collection

Squadron made a pin-point daylight attack at rooftop height on an art gallery in The Hague, Netherlands. The building was being used by the Gestapo to store the central registry of the Dutch population. The leading two aircraft dropped high explosive bombs to 'open up' the building, their bombs entering through the doors and windows. The following aircraft then dropped incendiary bombs, destroying the records and much of the rest of the building. Such was the accuracy of the bombing that nearby civilians were unharmed.

A major precision raid was also prosecuted on October 31, 1944, against the Gestapo headquarters offices located at the University of Aarhus in Denmark. The Danish

resistance, under pressure from the German authorities, requested the raid and the reliable 140 Wing was again called into action. Therefore on the morning of October 31, 24 Mosquito FB.VIs belonging to 140 Wing took off from RAF Swanton Morley in Norfolk, escorted by eight Mustangs from 315 (Polish) Squadron. They were accompanied by a camera-carrying Mosquito of the RAF's FPU. The attack was made by four waves of Mosquitos. The first aircraft 'opened up' the relevant buildings with high explosive bombs, while those following dropped incendiary bombs to start large fires.

Overall the raid was a success, with much of the Gestapo's documentation destroyed while two key secret agents who were being interrogated by the Gestapo managed to escape in the confusion. Sadly, several Danish civilians, including some construction workers were killed in one of the explosions. All the RAF aircraft survived, although one Mosquito was damaged and landed in nearby neutral Sweden.

Hazardous undertaking

Just weeks before the end of World War Two, on March 21, 1945 a similarly hazardous raid was carried out on a high-value and important target in the Danish capital, Copenhagen. Known as Operation Carthage, the Mosquito units involved again were 21, 464 and 487 Squadrons. The raid involved a very low-level bombing attack on the Gestapo headquarters in the 'Shell House' (Shellhus) near the centre of Copenhagen.

A raid on this significant location had been requested several times by the Danish resistance. Initially it was thought to be too dangerous, RAF recce photographs together with reports on the location by resistance members showing the target to be in a built-up area near to a school. Eventually, however, it was decided to go ahead, although the planned raid was always going to be risky for the aircrews involved, as well as local civilians. To ensure complete surprise, no warning could be given to the Danish population of the impending attack.

Twenty Mosquitoes from the three squadrons were involved, divided

into three attack waves. The first wave, flying just about as low as it was practicable, successfully located the Shellhus and attacked, placing several bombs onto the building. It was later estimated that this initial strike – together with the immediately following waves – killed some 55 Germans plus 47 Danes working for the Gestapo. Many Gestapo records were also destroyed. Unfortunately, some Danish prisoners of the Gestapo were also killed, but it was later revealed that several other Danes managed to escape from the debris.

However, a Mosquito from the first wave struck a tall lamp post and crashed in the vicinity of the nearby Catholic school. Overall the raid cost the attackers four Mosquitos and their crews, nine of which were fatalities.

The second wave of the attack was almost erred into mistaking the fire and smoke from this accident for the planned target. The third wave, however, apparently approaching from an unintended direction, came to the school first and most dropped their bombs onto it by mistake, killing more than 24 civilians together with eight teachers and 86 children.

Using both high explosive and incendiary bombs, the daring 140 Wing attack on the Gestapo facilities in Aarhus during October 1944 caused extensive damage, as photographed by one of the Mosquitos that took part. Malcolm V Lowe Collection

The daylight raid during December 1942 on the Philips factory at Eindhoven, Netherlands was an early baptism of fire for the Mosquito in pin-point raids, although the bombing was higher than the rooftop attacks of later in the war. This image shows an RAF aircraft, either a Mosquito or a Boston, over the target. JB via Malcolm V Lowe

Tony Agar's Mosquito during
ground running at East Kirkby.
All Key – Jamie Ewan

WALK AROUND

▲ The fairing unit and muzzles of the four 20mm Hispano cannon.

▲ Starboard carburettor air intake.

Mosquito NF.II HJ711 is the star of this volume's detail photo feature. The aircraft is owned by Tony Agar and resides at the Lincolnshire Aviation Heritage Centre, East Kirkby. It is unique as the only example of this variant in existence, and has been restored over almost 40 years to ground running condition by using parts from other Mosquito sub-types. For more information visit: www.lincsaviation.co.uk

▲ Note the rivet pattern on the port elevator.

▲ The port engine nacelle and propeller spinner.

WALK AROUND

The bomb bay doors, with spent cartridge ejector ports.

Perspex covers enclose each wing-tip navigation light. The port example is pictured here.

Tailwheel with towing arm attached.

Here's the detail of the port radiator unit.

Barrels of the four .303 machine guns, and the so-called 'bow and arrow' radar antenna.

The starboard landing light deployed.   Tail navigation lights.

▲ The navigator's seat is a basic affair.

◄ A peak through the access door provides a view of the busy instrument panel.

▼ A close-up of the throttle quadrant.

▼ A little more comfort is available on the pilot's seat.

▼ Rear mudguard on the starboard undercarriage.

▼ A side study of the starboard wheel and strut arrangement.

KITOGRAPHY

There has been a wealth of Mosquito kits, decals and accessories over the years. Many are still available and the most up-to-date item is Airfix's new-tool 1/72 Mosquito B.XVI, which has already prompted aftermarket firms to produce additional parts and markings. This list is not definitive, being more of a cross-section and representing items (mostly) available currently, while some can still be found on the second-hand market and at auction sites. Many of these products are available at www.hannants.co.uk

KITS

Mark I Models
(www.4pluspublications.com)

1/144

14483 DH Mosquito B.IV 'Wooden Bomber'

14484 DH Mosquito B.IV/PR.IV 'Swift Warrior'

14485 DH Mosquito B.VII/B.XX/F-8 'Canadian Mossie'

14494 DH Mosquito B.IV/PR.IV 'Special Liveries'

Airfix (www.airfix.com)

1/72

A04023 Mosquito B.XVI (new tool 2021)

A03019 Mosquito Mk.II/VI/XVIII

1/48

A07100 Mosquito FB.VI

A07112 Mosquito B.XVI/PR.XVI

A07112 Mosquito PR.XVI

1/24

A25001 Mosquito NF.II/FB.VI

A25001A Mosquito FB.VI

Hasegawa (www.amerang.co.uk)

1/72

HCP17 Mosquito B.IV

Hong Kong Models
(www.bachmann.co.uk)

1/32

01E015 Mosquito B.IV Series II

01E016 Mosquito B Mk.IX/Mk.XVI

Matchbox

1/72

PK-116 Mosquito Mk.IX/NF.30

Revell (www.revell.de/en)

1/32

4758 Mosquito Mk.IV

Tamiya (www.hobbyco.net)

1/72

60747 Mosquito Mk.VI/NF.II

60753 Mosquito B.IV/PR.Mk.IV

60765 Mosquito NF.XIII/XVII

1/48

61062 Mosquito FB.VI/NF.II

61066 Mosquito B.IV/PR.IV

1/32

60326 Mosquito FB.VI

ACCESSORIES

Aires (www.aires.cz)

1/72

7067 FB.VI/NF.II Cockpit Set (Tamiya)

7077 FB.VI/NF.II Detail Set (Tamiya)

7091 FB.VI/NF.II Gun Bay (Tamiya)

7099 FB.VI/NF.II Bomb Bay (Tamiya)

7154 Wheels + Paint Mask (Tamiya)

1/48

4086 FB.VI/NF.II Cockpit Set (Tamiya)

4152 FB.VI Bomb Bay (Tamiya)

4177 FB.VI Gun Bay (Tamiya)

4200 FB.VI/NF.II Engine Set (Tamiya)

4208 FB.VI/NF.II Wheel Bay (Tamiya)

4294 Wheels + Paint Mask (Tamiya)

4296 Wheels + Paint Mask (Tamiya)

4463 B.IV Cockpit Set (Tamiya)

Airwaves (www.hannants.co.uk)

1/72

AC72166 Mk.II/VI/XVIII (Airfix)

**Alley Cat Models (www.alleycatmodels.
co.uk / www.modelsforsale.com)**

1/72

72044C B.IV Series I Conversion (Tamiya)

1/32

32044C Mosquito Block Tread Tyres

1/24

24005C TR.33 Sea Mosquito Conversion
(decals)

24005C TR.33 Sea Mosquito Conversion
(masks)

24006C Mosquito FB.XVIII 'Tse-Tse'
Conversion (decals)

24006C Mosquito FB.XVIII 'Tse-Tse'
Conversion (masks)

24009C Sea Mosquito Wing Fold
Conversion

Armory (www.armorymodels.com)

1/72

72406 DH.98 Mosquito Weighted Wheels

1/48

48402 DH.98 Mosquito Weighted Wheels

Airscale (www.airscale.co.uk)

1/24

24 MOSA Mosquito NF.II/FB.VI Instrument
Panel (Airfix)

24 BEZ German, RAF and US Instrument
Bezels

PE24 DET German, RAF and US Cockpit
Details

Attack Squadron (www.attacksquadron.pl)

1/72

72067 TR1143 Radio Set

**Barracuda Studios (www.barracudacast.
com)**

1/32

BR32262 Mosquito WWII Radio Upgrade

BR32265 FB.VI Ammo Feed Chutes

BR32267 FB.VI Rocker Covers

1/24

24281 Late Mainwheels

**Blackbird Models (www.blackbirdmodels.
co.uk)**

1/72

BMA72043 Mosquito T.III conversion

BMA72051 Mosquito 100gal Tanks

BMA72047 Mosquito FB.VI ASH Radar

BMA72006 Mosquito Highball Conversion

1/48

BMA48001 Mosquito NF.XII nose
conversion (Tamiya)

Black Dog (www.blackdog-model.com)

A72050 Mosquito Mk.VI Set No.1
(Tamiya)

A72051 Mosquito Mk.VI Set No.2
(Tamiya)

A72052 Mosquito MK.VI Big Set (Tamiya)

Brengun (www.brengun.cz)

1/144

Mosquito wheels (B.IV/PR.IV/PR.V.VII/B.
XX/F-8)

1/72

72171 Mosquito two-stage Merlin engine
nacelles set (Tamiya)

72207 Mosquito wheels block pattern
(Tamiya)

1/48

48124 Mosquito two-stage Merlin engine
nacelles (Tamiya)

CMK (www.cmkkits.com)

1/72

7036 Engine Set (Hasegawa)

7037 Interior (Hasegawa)

7038 Control Surfaces (Hasegawa)

7047 Mk.IV Detail Set (Hasegawa)

7105 PR.XVI Conversion (Tamiya)

7116 Mk.IV Armament (Hasegawa)

7227 FB.VI Bomb Bay (Tamiya)

7228 B.IV Exterior (Tamiya)

7229 B.IV Control Surfaces (Tamiya)

7267 Packard V-1650-7

Q72024 Mk.IV/VI Oil Coolers

1/48

4036 Interior (Tamiya)

4038 RR Merlin Engine (Tamiya)

4106 Mk.IV/VI Exterior (Tamiya)

4108 Two-stage Merlin Conversion
(Tamiya)

4241 Wing-Mounted Coolers (Tamiya)

4260 Mk.II/IV/VI Control Surfaces (Tamiya)

Q48114 Tail Strut (Tamiya)

Q48193 Hispano Mk.II Cannon

Eduard (www.eduard.com)

1/72

CX119 Mosquito Fighter Canopy Mask
(Tamiya)

CX121 Mosquito Bomber Canopy Mask
(Tamiya)

CX164 Mosquito Canopy Mask
(Hasegawa)

SS137 Mosquito Mk.VI (Tamiya)

1/48

49239 FB.VI/NF.II (Tamiya)

49242 B.IV/PR.IV (Tamiya)

49438 B.IV Interior (Tamiya)

EX028 Mk.IV Canopy Mask (Tamiya)

EX029 FB.VI/NF.II Canopy Mask (Tamiya)

EX268 B.IV Canopy Mask (Revell)

FE239 FB.VI/NF.II (Tamiya)

FE242 B.IV/PR.IV (Tamiya)

FE438 B.IV Interior SA (Revell)

1/32

32376 Mk.IV Bomb Bay (Hong Kong Models)

32377 Mk.IV Exterior/Engines (Hong Kong Models)

32379 FB.VI Exterior (Tamiya)

32839 Mk.IV Fabric Seatbelts (Hong Kong Models)

32840 Mk.IV Interior SA (Hong Kong Models)

32841 Mk.IV Seatbelts (Hong Kong Models)

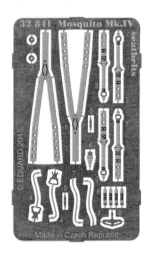

32845 FB.VI Seatbelts (Tamiya)

32846 FB.VI Fabric Seatbelts (Tamiya)

32849 FB.VI Interior (Tamiya)

33148 Mk.IV Interior (Hong Kong Models)

33151 FB.VI Interior (Tamiya)

632061 Mk.IV Wheels (Hong Kong Models)

632062 Mk.IV Exhaust Stacks (Hong Kong Models)

632065 Mk.VI Wheels (Tamiya)

632066 Mk.VI Exhaust Stacks (Tamiya)

632077 FB.VI Nose Guns (Tamiya)

632078 FB.VI Gun Bay (Tamiya)

632090 FB.VI Engines (Tamiya)

632091 FB.VI Right Engine (Tamiya)

632092 FB.VI Left Engine (Tamiya)

63210 Mosquito FB.VI Big Sin set (Tamiya)

BIG3355 Mk.IV

BIG3359 Mk.VI

JX182 Mk.IV Canopy Mask (Hong Kong Models)

JX184 FB.VI Canopy Mask (Tamiya)

SIN63208 Mk.IV (Hong Kong Models)

1/24

23005 RAF WWII Seat Belts Early

23006 RAF WWII Seat Belts Late

Falcon Models (www.falconmodels.co.nz)

1/72

Set 2 RAF Fighters World War II

Set 8 RAF Bomber World War II (Part 1)

Set 17 RAF World War II Part 2

1/48

Set 31 RAF Fighters World War II

Set 40 RAF Part 2

Freightdog (www.freightdogmodels.co.uk)

1/72

Mosquito B.XVI (H2S) conversion (Set 2) for Airfix new tool

Mosquito B.XVI/B.35 Improvements (Set 1) for Airfix new tool

1/48

Mosquito PR.34 (Early) conversion (Airfix)

HGW Models (www.hgwmodels.cz)

1/48

148543 Seatbelts

1/32

132809 Mk.VI Seatbelts and Canopy Mask (Tamiya)

132568 Mk.VI Seatbelts (Tamiya)

1/24

124505 Sutton QK Harness (RAF) Seatbelts

124509 Seatbelts (Airfix)

Kits World (www.kitsworld.co.uk)

1/48

3D 1481025 Mosquito B Mk.,IV/PR Mk.IV 3D instrument panel decal

3D 1481026 Mosquito FB Mk.VI 3D instrument panel decal

1/32

3D 1321029 Mosquito B Mk.,IV/PR Mk.IV 3D instrument panel decal

3D 1321030 Mosquito FB Mk.VI 3D instrument panel decal

LF Models (www.lfmodels.com)

1/72

M7217 Mk.VI Camouflage Mask (Airfix, Hasegawa, Tamiya)

M7218 Mk.IV Camouflage Mask Part 1 (Airfix, Hasegawa, Tamiya)

M7219 Mk.IV Camouflage Mask Part 2 (Airfix, Hasegawa, Tamiya)

1/48

M4815 Mk.VI Camouflage Mask (Airfix/ Tamiya)

M4816 Mk.IV Camouflage Mask Part 1 (Revell/Monogram/Tamiya/Airfix)

M4817 Mk.IV Camouflage Mask Part 2 (Revell/Monogram/Tamiya/Airfix)

Maestro Models (www.maestromodels.com)

1/72

MMK7278 4-Blade Propellers

1/48

MMK4880 4-Blade Propellers

1/24

MMK2401 Mk.XIX nose SwAF J30 (Airfix)

Master Model (www.master-model.pl)

1/72

AM-72-091 NF.II/FB.VI Pitot and Armament

1/48

AM-48-026 British Mk.2 Browning .303 Caliber

AM-48-111 NF.II/FB.VI Pitot and Armament

1/32

AM-32-083 NF.II/FB.VI Pitot and Armament (Tamiya)

1/24

AM-24-001 British Mk.2 Browning .303 Caliber

AM-24-004 Hispano Mk.II 20mm Cannon

AM-24-011 British 3in Rocket RP-3 with 60lb SAP Heads (Early)

AM-24-012 British 3in Rocket RP-3 with 60lb SAP Heads (Late)

Montex (www.montex-mask.com)

1/72

72014 Canopy Mask (Tamiya)

72068 Mk.VI Canopy Mask (Hasegawa)

72069 Mk.IV Canopy Mask (Tamiya)

1/48

48173 NF.II/FB.VI Canopy and Markings Mask (Tamiya)

48174 FB.VI Canopy and Markings Mask (Tamiya)

48283 Mk.IV Canopy and Markings Mask (Tamiya)

48322 FB.VI Canopy and Markings Mask (Tamiya)

48004 NF.II/FB.VI Canopy and Markings Mask (Tamiya)

48230 Mk.XVI Canopy and Markings Mask (Airfix)

48241 Mk.IV Canopy and Markings Mask (Tamiya)

48306 Mk.IV Canopy and Markings Mask (Revell)

48004 NF.II/FB.VI Canopy (Tamiya)

48228 FB.VI Canopy Mask (Airfix)

48230 Mk.XVI Canopy Mask (Airfix)

48241 Mk.IV Canopy Mask (Tamiya)

48306 Mk.IV Canopy Mask (Revell)

1/32

32297 Mk.IV Canopy and Markings Mask (Revell)

32322 FB.VI Canopy and Markings Mask (Tamiya)

32329 FB.VI Canopy and Markings Mask (Tamiya)

32163 Mk.VI Canopy and Markings Mask (Tamiya)

32060 Mk.IV Canopy Mask (Revell)

32162 Mk.IV/PR.I/IV Canopy Mask (Hong Kong Models)

32163 FB.VI Canopy Mask (Tamiya)

1/24

24051 NF.II/FB.VI Canopy and Markings Mask

24079 NF.II/FB.VI Canopy and Markings Mask

24015 NF.II/FB.VI Canopy and Markings Mask

24015 NF.II/FB.VI Canopy Mask

Pavla Models (www.pavlamodels.cz)

1/72

C72038 T.III Cockpit (Tamiya)

C72046 B.IV Cockpit (Tamiya)

U72060 Mk.IV Bomb Bay (Tamiya)

U72062 RR Merlin 73/72 engine cowlings (Tamiya)

V72-09 Mosquito (Fighter) Canopy (Airfix)

Peewit (www.peewit-modely.cz)

1/144

Mosquito B.IV/PR.IV canopy masks (Mark I)

Pmask

1/32

32004 Mosquito Mk.IV/Mk.VI RAF National Insignia paint masks

Airfix's new-tool 1/72 Mosquito B.XVI, built for *Airfix Model World* by David Holmes.

Profimodeller (www.profimodeller.com)

1/32

P32173 UK/US HVAR Rocket (Tamiya/Revell)

P32241 Pitot Tube (Hong Kong Models)

P32242 Bomb Bay (Hong Kong Models)

P32243 Interior (Hong Kong Models)

Quickboost (www.aires.cz)

1/72

72121 Undercarriage Covers (Tamiya)

72204 FB.VI Nose (Tamiya)

72301 Exhaust (Tamiya)

72425 Oil Radiators (Tamiya)

72550 Mosquito seats with safety belts (Tamiya)

72606 Mosquito NF.XII radar cover (Tamiya)

1/48

48030 Sea Mosquito Conversion Set (Tamiya)

48140 Undercarriage Covers (Tamiya)

48252 FB.VI Nose (Tamiya)

48306 Exhaust (Tamiya)

48325 Wheel Fenders (Tamiya)

48593 Mk.IV Seats w/Safety Belts (Tamiya)

RB Productions (www.radubstore.com)

1/32

32016 Sutton QK Harness

32040 Mosquito Radiators

1/24

24001 Sutton QK Harness

24003 Mosquito Radiators

Rob-Taurus (www.rob-taurus.cz)

1/72

72071 Mk.II/VI (Tamiya)

72072 B.IV/PR.IV (Tamiya)

1/48

48068 Mk.II/VI (Tamiya)

48069 B.IV/PR.IV (Tamiya)

Scale Aircraft Conversions (www.scaleaircraftconversions.com)

1/48

48038 Landing Gear (Tamiya)

1/32

32099 Landing Gear (Tamiya)

1/24

24002 Landing Gear (Airfix)

Squadron (www.squadron.com)

1/72

9156 Mk.VI canopy (Airfix)

1/48

9532 FB.VI (Airfix)

9600 FB.VI (Tamiya)

Topnotch (www.topnotch-success.net)

1/72

TNM72-M30 Mk.IV/VI Camouflage Mask

1/48

TNM48-M30 Mk.IV/VI Camouflage Mask

1/32

TNM32-M30 Mk.IV/VI Camouflage Mask

1/24

TNM24-M30 Mk.IV/VI Camouflage Mask

Ultracast (www.ultracast.ca)

1/48

48001 500lb MC Mk.III British General Purpose Bombs

48002 1000lb MC Mk.I British General Purpose Bombs

48033 Seats (late pattern)

48034 Control Surfaces

48035 FB.VI Crew Access Door (Tamiya)

48045 Tail Wheel (Tamiya)

48046 Mud Guards (Tamiya)

48047 Flame Dampening Exhaust Shrouds (Tamiya)

48048 FB.VI AI Mk.XV ASH Radar Nose (Tamiya)

48104 5-Stack Exhausts (Tamiya)

48118 100 gal Fuel Tanks (Tamiya)

48246 Spoked Wheels Block Tread

48247 Standard Wheels Block Tread

48248 Spoked Wheels Diamond Tread

48249 Standard Wheels Diamond Tread

48250 Standard Wheels Australian Z-Block Tread

Valom (www.valom.net)

1/48

DSV02 B.IX/B.XVI/PR.34 Conversion (Tamiya)

Yahu Models (www.yahumodels.siemianowice.com)

1/72

7260 NF.II/FB.VI Instrument Panel (Hasegawa/Tamiya)

1/48

YMA4830 NF.II/FB.VI Instrument Panel (Tamiya)

1/32

3210 NF.II/FB.VI Instrument Panel (Tamiya)

1/24

2411 Mosquito FB.VI instrument panel (Airfix)

DECALS

Aviaeology (www.aviaeology.com)

1/72

AOD72005M RCAF 418 Sqn

AOD72023 Banff Strike Wing Mosquitoes (143, 235, 248 Sqns)

AOD72033 Coastal Strike Wing Outriders 333 Sqn (RNoAF) NF.II/FB.VI 1943-45

AOD72S05 FB.VI airframe/stencil data

1/48

AOD48005M RCAF FB.VI 418 Sqn Intruders

AOD48023 Banff Strike Wing (143, 235, 248 Sqns)

AOD32033 Coastal Strike Wing Outriders 333 Sqn (RNoAF) NF.II/FB.VI 1943-45

AOD48S05 FB.VI airframe/stencil data

1/32

AOD32005M RCAF FB.VI

AOD32011 RCAF FB.VI

AOD320231 Banff Strike Wing (143, 235, 248 Sqns) Pt.1

AOD320232 Banff Strike Wing (143, 235, 248 Sqns) Pt.2

AOD32033 Coastal Strike Wing Outriders 333 Sqn (RNoAF) NF.II/FB.VI 1943-45

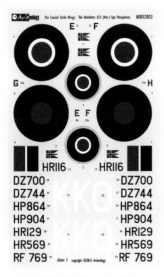

AOD32S05 FB.VI airframe/stencil data

1/24

AOD24005M RCAF NF.II/FB.VI

AOD24023 Banff Strike Wing (143, 235, 248 Sqns)

AOD24033 Coastal Strike Wing Outriders 333 Sqn (RNoAF) NF.II/FB.VI 1943-45

AOD24S05 NF.II/FB.VI airframe/stencil data part 1

Airscale (www.airscale.co.uk)

1/24

AS24 MOSA NF.II/FB.VI Instrument Panel

Avalon (www.avalondecals.com)

1/72

7042 Mosquito NF Mk.XII

Barracuda Studios (www.barracudacals.com)

1/72

BC72008 Stencil data for all marks

BC72165 Airframe Stencils – Expanded

1/48

BC48166 Airframe Stencils – Expanded

1/24

BC21467 Airframe Stencils – Expanded

Berna Decals (xbpro@aol.com)

1/72

BD 72-99 FB.VI in French and Foreign Service

1/48

BD 48-121 FB.VI in French and Foreign Service

1/32

BD 32-39 FB.VI in French Service

1/24

BD 24-02 FB.VI in French Service

Blackbird Models (www.blackbirdmodels.co.uk)

1/72

72017 Operation Overlord (PR.XVI)

72019 Post War RAF Part 1 (NF.36)

72025 DH Mosquito Pt.1 (PR.IX/B.IX/FB.VI)

72026 DH Mosquito Pt.2 (B.XVI/B.IV/NF.30/NF.XV)

72036 USAAF at War Pt.1 (B.XVI)

1/48

BMD 48008 Operation Overlord (PR.XVI)

Caracal Models (www.caracalmodels.com)

1/48

48183 USAAF Mosquitos

Carpena Decals (www.decals-carpena.com)

1/72

7230 Mosquito Part 1 (NF.II/NF.30/FB.VI/PR.XVI)

7231 Mosquito Part 2 (FB.VI/PR.XVI)

1/48

4822 Mosquito Part 1 (NF.II/FB.VI/PR.XVI)

4896 Mosquito Part 2 (FB.VI/PR.XVI)

4897 Mosquito Part 3 (NF.30/FB.VI)

Colorado (www.coloradodecals.com)

1/72

72.30 NF.II

72.31 Mk.VI

1/48

48022 Mosquito Part 1 (NF.II/FB.VI/PR.XVI)

48096 Mosquito Part 2 (FB.VI/PR.XVI)

48097 Mosquito Part 3 (NF.30/FB.VI)

DK Decals (www.dkdecals.cz)

1/72

72013 Mosquito in Czechoslovakian AF (NF.II/B.XXV/NF.XVII/NF.XII/NF.XIX/NF.30/PR.IX/PR.XVI/FB.VI/T.III)

72016 No.100 Group RAF (B.IV/FB.VI)

72060 Night Intruders Pt.1

72068 Night Intruders Pt.2

1/48

48005 Mosquito Australian pilots in RAAF and RAF (FB.VI/PR.40/PR.XVI/NF.XVII)

48007 Mosquito in Czechoslovakian AF (NF.II/NF.XVII/NF.XIX/NF.30/PR.IX/PR.XVI/FB.VI/T.III)

48009 No.100 Group RAF (B.IV/FB.VI)

1/32

32011 B-36 Mosquito in CzAF

32017 Mosquito PR Mk.IX/Mk.XVI of Czechoslovak Airmen

32018 Mosquito in RAAF Service

Dutch Decal (www.dutchdecal.nl)

1/32

32001 Dutchies in the RAF

Eagle Cal (www.eagle-editions.com)

1/72

72 167 B.IV/PR.IV

72 168 FB.VI

72 169 FB.VI

1/48

48 167 B.IV/PR.IV

48 168 FB.VI

48 169 FB.VI

1/32

32 167 B.IV/PR.IV

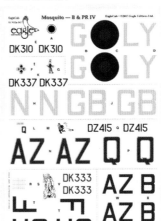

32 168 FB.VI

32 169 FB.VI

Freightdog (www.freightdogmodels.co.uk)

1/72

72-003S Weekend Warriors RAuxAF (T.3)

FSD72-004S Post War Brits Abroad Pt.II (FB.6)

1/48

FSD48-005 Post War Mosquitos in RAF Service (PR.34/B.35/NF.36)

FSD48-007 RAF Over Malaya 1948-1955 (PR.34A)

Fündekals :) (www.fundekals.com)

1/72

F-8 43-324926 'The Spook', 3rd Photographic Group (Reconnaissance), 12th AF, La Marsa, Tunisia, November 1943

1/48

F-8 43-324926 'The Spook', 3rd Photographic Group (Reconnaissance), 12th AF, La Marsa, Tunisia, November 1943

1/32

BOAC PR.IV

BOAC FB.VI

HGW (www.hgwmodels.cz)

1/48

248022 Stencils (Wet Transfers)

1/32

232011 FB.VI Stencils (Wet Transfers)

Iliad Design (www.iliad-design.com)

1/48

48023 Canadian-built Mosquitos (B.XX/B.VII/FB.26)

IsraDecal Studio (www.isradecal.com)

1/48